SEYCHELLES

SOMALIA
INDIAN
OCEAN
KENYA
SEYCHELLES
Victoria
TANZANIA
COMOROS
MOZAMBIQUE
MADAGASCAR
MAURITIUS

www.marco-polo.com

← INSIDE FRONT COVER: THE BEST HIGHLIGHTS

The best Insider Tips → p. 4

Best of ... → p. 6

Mahé → p. 32

Praslin/Neighbouring islands → p. 52

SYMBOLS

- INSIDER TIP — Insider Tip
- ★ — Highlight
- ●●●● — Best of ...
- Scenic view
- Responsible travel: fair trade principles and the environment respected

PRICE CATEGORIES HOTELS

Expensive	over 4000 rupees
Moderate	2500–4000 rupees
Budget	under 2500 rupees

The prices are for two people in a double room per night including breakfast (no seasonal supplements)

PRICE CATEGORIES RESTAURANTS

Expensive	over 500 rupees
Moderate	325–500 rupees
Budget	under 325 rupees

The prices are valid for a meal with starter, main course and dessert but exclude drinks

On the cover: Hike through lush tropical forests p. 63 | Exotic fruits & fragrant spices p. 37

CONTENTS

Bird & Denis Island → p. 68

Silhouette & North Island → p. 74

Outer Seychelles → p. 80

Road atlas → p. 114

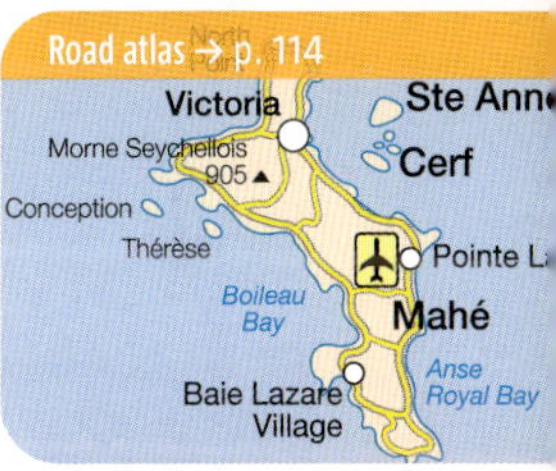

DID YOU KNOW?

MAPS IN THE GUIDEBOOK

(116 A1) Page numbers and coordinates refer to the road atlas
(0) Site/address located off the map
Coordinates are also given for places that are not marked on the road atlas
A street map of Victoria (Mahé) can be found inside the back cover

INSIDE BACK COVER: PULL-OUT MAP →

PULL-OUT MAP

(A–B 2–3) Refers to the removable pull-out map

The best MARCO POLO Insider Tips

Our top 15 Insider Tips

INSIDER TIP Window to the sea

Enjoy the fantastic underwater world without getting wet: on La Digue the owner of the Bernique Guesthouse organises excursions in a glass bottom boat → p. 59

INSIDER TIP Milkshakes with a difference

At the Frangipani bistro in Quatre Bornes, in the south of Mahé, they serve milkshakes with rather unusual flavours – try one! → p. 90

INSIDER TIP Cheap and tasty

At the Boathouse on Mahé you can feast until all the dishes are empty: delicious Creole cuisine, buffet style → p. 45

INSIDER TIP Atmosphere and tradition

Set in verdant tropical gardens with magnificent views of the ocean, Le Méridien Fisherman's Cove on Mahé has been renovated and is now a discretely luxurious five star resort → p. 46

INSIDER TIP Spices for a king

Le Jardin du Roi (king's garden) was originally created to compete with the Asian Spice Islands → p. 47

INSIDER TIP Handicrafts made in Seychelles

In the Vilaz Artizanal (craft village) on Mahé, souvenir hunters will find a wide selection of the country's handicraft products on offer. Stroll around the small, neat wooden huts and watch the artisans at work as they make decorative items such as batik and pottery (photo above) → p. 48

INSIDER TIP Life in the coral reef

Full of colourful fish: the varied marine life in the coral reefs off Praslin (photo right) makes for ideal snorkelling conditions → p. 67

INSIDER TIP Fresh from the shell

On Praslin pearl oysters are cultivated and jewellery pieces made of the fine black (!) pearls are also sold → p. 63

INSIDER TIP The sign of Capricorn

Capricorn Restaurant on Praslin might be a little out of the way, but the detour to Anse Kerlan is definitely worth it. It is popular for its seafood and Creole dishes and well known for its delicious home-made sorbets → p. 63

INSIDER TIP Invasion of the terns

It feels a little like Alfred Hitchcock's world-famous cult shocker 'The Birds', when millions of birds swoop on to Bird Island → p. 70

INSIDER TIP Beware, carnivores!

Interesting not only to botanists: the extremely rare carnivorous pitcher plants can still be found on Silhouette Island → p. 77

INSIDER TIP Petting zoo without a fence

Here you can observe animals in the wild: on the small neighbouring islands of Praslin you will be able to get close to rare birds and reptiles → p. 97

INSIDER TIP From the bush to the cup

Pay a visit to the Tea Factory – the only tea plantation in the Seychelles – and relax with a cup of tea (or two) and recover from your hike up Morne Blanc on Mahé. If you are still able, you can take a guided tour of the facilities, which have been in operation for over 50 years → p. 40, 91

INSIDER TIP The Arabs are coming!

While Arab seafarers are a thing of the past, you can still enjoy an exciting Arabian horseback ride on the main island of Mahé (or on La Digue) – a great experience for those who are passionate about riding → p. 95

INSIDER TIP Giants of the ocean

They only want to play: harmless whale sharks are the giants of the oceans and if you take a guided dive you may just get lucky – they are in Seychelles waters between October and April → p. 95

BEST OF ...

GREAT PLACES FOR FREE

Discover new places and save money

FOR FREE

● ***Market spectacle***

Victoria's vibrant and bustling *Sir Selwyn Selwyn Clarke Market* is open daily from 6am. If you arrive at this time, you can watch as the traders set up their fruit, vegetables, spices and fresh fish and then serve their first customers → p. 37

● ***Beautiful jewellery and beautiful paintings***

You can get a good (and free) overview of the artistic work of the many painters and sculptors in the Seychelles at *Kenwyn House* on Francis Rachel Street in Victoria → p. 36

● ***Something to snack on***

Sightseeing in the capital Victoria will make you a little peckish. Take a break at one of the small takeaway restaurants in the city centre. From about 11 am there are Creole dishes at low prices (about 40 rupees) → p. 27

● ***The beaches are for everyone***

On the Seychelles there is a law that stipulates that all beaches (photo) must be accessible to everyone. This includes the beaches that belong to exclusive hotels, such as the *Banyan Tree* at the Anse Intendance on Mahé. Even if you don't stay there, no one will look at you strangely should you wish to visit the beach (for free) → p. 49

● ***A test dive***

The underwater world off the Seychelles is considered to be one of the most beautiful diving sites on earth. If you want to know how you fare with a mask and snorkel, you can do a trial course on Mahé with the *Underwater Centre* at Beau Vallon Bay → p. 38

● ***Across the island on a bike***

You can explore the island of La Digue for just a few rupees when you hire a bicycle from *La Digue Island Lodge*. The bike is the best mode of transport on the island, and bike thieves are virtually unknown because everyone already owns one ... → p. 59

ONLY ON THE SEYCHELLES

Unique experiences

• *Off to church!*

The Seychellois know how to celebrate and even a Sunday church attendance is a celebration – men and women come clad in colourful and festive outfits (photo). A highlight not to be missed: the procession for the Feast of Assumption on La Digue → p. 98

• *Guests of Marie Antoinette*

The Creole cuisine is varied and always fresh! One of the most recommended restaurants is *Marie Antoinette* on Mahé, where they have new lunch and dinner menus daily. And because everything is bought fresh at the market, you can be sure that each course on the menu will be a delight! → p. 39

• *A visit to the 'Gauguin of the Seychelles'*

What you also shouldn't miss is a visit to Sir Michael Adams, the Seychelles' most famous painter. His house at Anse aux Poules Bleues on Mahé is surrounded by lush greenery and quite well hidden. If the artist is not available in person, his wife Heather is the right person to speak to → p. 46

• *A coco de mer for the mantelpiece?*

Typical of the Seychelles is the coco de mer, the sea coconut. There is hardly any other fruit on earth that is as steeped in myth as this palm (indigenous to the Seychelles) with its large, heavy nut → p. 18

• *Exploring Aride on foot*

Each Seychelles island has its own botanical and ornithological specialities and this certainly applies to Aride and you can explore the nature reserve on a round trip from Praslin. Its feature is that it has one of the highest densities of lizards in the world → p. 53

• *Giant tortoises*

Once thought to be extinct, their numbers have steadily increased and they are now once again found on many of the islands in the Seychelles. Many of these impressive giant tortoises don't mind being handled, such as Caspar and Caroline on Cerf Island → p. 42

BEST OF ...

AND IF IT RAINS?

Activities to brighten your day

Browse old books

The history of the Seychelles may not be that old but old books have many stories to tell. That's why it is worth paying the *National Library* in Victoria a visit on a rainy day. The archive includes some special collections and it is very well organised → p. 36

Hiking under nature's umbrella

Hard to believe yet true: a hike through the unique *Vallée de Mai* on Praslin is also an adventure you can undertake in (light) rain. The trees and palms are so dense that the huge leaf fronds serve as the perfect canopy to keep the raindrops at bay. No matter what the weather, sturdy hiking boots are essential → p. 63

In the footsteps of the first islanders

The National Museum, in the centre of Victoria on Mahé, is dedicated to the historical heritage of the Seychelles. There you can view some interesting exhibits that include documents about the history of the settlement of the Seychelles, historic nautical charts, models of ships and much more → p. 36

Pause for a few minutes

You don't need to be a Hindu in order to enter the Arul Mihu Navasakthi Vinayagar Hindu temple. You can escape a rain shower during a walk through Victoria by spending a few minutes respectfully observing the Hindu ceremonies (photo) → p. 36

Dine when it rains

What can be more romantic than dinner by candlelight with the sound of soft music and the patter of rain outside? One such atmospheric setting is *La Scala* restaurant at North Point on Mahé → p. 45

RELAX AND CHILL OUT

Take it easy and spoil yourself

● ***Relax in fragrant herbs***

The spa at the *Four Seasons* hotel on Mahé offers wellness at its finest: their scrubs, wraps and treatments make use of local flowers, herbs and spices and traditional recipes → p. 50

● ***Hang out and chill***

The *Pirates Arms*, not far from the Clock Tower in Victoria's city centre, is a popular place so it may take a while for your chilled local ale to arrive at your table but just relax, kick back, see and be seen. The best seating is in the area at the front → p. 39

● ***Improve your handicap***

There are two golf courses in the Seychelles, one with nine holes on Mahé and one with 18 holes on Praslin (photo). The latter at Anse Kerlan is the nicer of the two, with some spectacular views of the Indian Ocean, a treat for the eyes and the senses → p. 66, 94

● ***The sun salute***

There is one sure cure for sensory overload: yoga! Relax, de-stress, balance the mind and body and find your inner peace with only a few minutes of yoga every day. At the *Maia Luxury Resort* on Mahé you can do so under expert guidance → p. 50

● ***Relax at reasonable prices***

The spa at the *Black Parrot Suites* in the *Coco de Mer Hotel* on Praslin is brand new and the prices for treatments are quite reasonable. The massage oils are tailor-made to suit the individual – after an analysis of one's karma. Until now, a real insider tip! → p. 65

● ***Picture-perfect beach***

The perfect beach to daydream on – it really is truly idyllic – can be found at Anse Mondon on Silhouette Island. From La Passe the hike takes just over an hour, but as a reward you can relax and stretch out on the sand and listen to the murmur of the waves → p. 76

INTRODUCTION

DISCOVER THE SEYCHELLES!

This much is clear: there is so much more to the Seychelles than its exquisite beaches – it is not just a travel destination for sunbathing and lounging around. The magic of these Indian Ocean islands is multifaceted: the lush tropical vegetation, the exceptional flora and fauna and – last but not least – the friendly, fun-loving people that make a trip to this archipelago off the African coast an unforgettable experience. According to geologists, the largest part of the archipelago is a scattered remnant of the ancient continent of Gondwana. The Seychelles Inner Islands, including the main island of Mahé, are made of granite, which towers up to heights of over 900m/2950ft above sea level and drops off sharply at the coast in bizarrely shaped cliffs and reefs. These rocks are merely the visible tip of a giant underwater mountain range, the Mahé Plateau. Over the course of centuries some coralline islands and reefs also formed,

Photo: Anse Takamaka on Mahé

making this area famous amongst divers and snorkellers. Stretching far out from the Mahé Plateau is another mighty underwater ridge made of volcanic basalt. This is where the Outer Islands are; a group of coralline islands with fine, white sand. They differ from the granite islands in that they are very flat with raised coral reefs. If you take all 115 islands together, you would have a surface area of 180 square miles. Mahé at 60 square miles is the largest (and most densely populated) island of the Seychelles.

Arab seafarers were the first to set foot on the Seychelles. Around AD 800 they discovered the archipelago on their trade voyages to India. Portuguese seafarers followed suit and in 1502 Vasco da Gama sighted the islands known as the Amirantes, southwest of Mahé. In the 16th/17th century, pirates and buccaneers arrived, most notably the legendary Olivier Levasseur, who called himself 'La Buse' (The Buzzard). He is believed to have buried a vast treasure, before his death by hanging on Mahé, and the booty is still being searched for by treasure hunters to this day. The Seychelles have kept their current name since 1756, when the Irish Captain Corneille Nicolas Morphey took possession of the islands under the orders of the French Crown. They were named after Jean Moreau de Sechelles, Louis XV's finance minister.

Playground for seafarers and pirates

There are plenty of dazzling personalities in the history of the Seychelles, such as the Frenchman Quéau de Quinssy, who took over as Governor in 1794. When the British arrived in Victoria with massive superior military forces on 16 May of that year, de Quinssy saw no other option but to sign a capitulation certificate that he had drafted himself. But no sooner had the British ships disappeared over the horizon,

Around AD 800
Arab seafarers land in the Seychelles

1502/03
Vasco da Gama discovers the Seychelles en route to India

From 1685
Pirates use the island as a hideout

1756
The Irish Captain Corneille N. Morphey declares Mahé a French colony

1770
French settlers establish the first settlement on Ste Anne

1794–1811
Chevalier Quéau de Quinssy, the island's

Exciting encounter whilst snorkelling: eye to eye with a magnificent turtle

than de Quinssy took down the Union Jack and hoisted the Tricolour again. Until 1811 this game was apparently repeated seven times. The annexation of the Seychelles by the British was ultimately unavoidable and in 1833 the new masters abolished slavery. Decades later the nation finally gained independence and on the outskirts of Victoria on Mahé there is a monument that marks this landmark event. The *Zonm Lib* is the statue of a man symbolically breaking free of his chains.

Vibrant republic in the Indian Ocean

Today the Repiblik Sesel (the official Creole name for the Republic of the Seychelles) is regarded as a relatively stable democracy, one which usually has a socialist-leaning head of state. On the 5th June 1977 the Prime Minister France Albert René took advantage of the democratically elected President James R. Mancham's absence and staged a coup d'etat. From then on René, who studied in Switzerland and England,

Commandant, surrenders eight times to the British, but hoists the French flag repeatedly after their departure

1811 The British annex the islands and prohibit slavery in 1833

From 1875 The Seychelles becomes a place of exile

1903 The British government declares the Seychelles a Crown colony

1964 The Seychelles Democratic Party (SDP) and the Seychelles People's United Party (SPUP) are founded

won all the elections – he effectively ran a one-party state until 1993 – without any opposition to challenge him. But even after 1993, when multiple parties were allowed to participate, René always emerged victorious at the polls. In 2004 he stepped down and handed his office over to his Vice President, James Alix Michel, who was re-elected in 2006 and 2011.

It would appear that it is of little concern to many Seychellois who heads up the country's parliament. Live and let live is their motto. This attitude is possible because the government provides a social system with free education and primary care in sickness and old age. A further contributing factor is that the standard of living in the Seychelles is considerably higher than in continental Africa. However, the cost of living has risen dramatically in recent years, and many Seychellois now only manage to cope financially by taking on a second job. It is interesting to note that the state provides more than half of the 30,000 jobs in the economy. And the balance of trade deficit is well establish because the Seychelles has little in the way of significant foreign exchange reserves and a large part of their revenue from tourism has to be reinvested in the import of items such as food.

Fishing, spice trade and tourism

The opening of the international airport on Mahé in 1972 heralded the beginning of organised tourism, which today represents the main source of income, generating about 70 per cent of state revenue while fishing and fish processing and the spice trade play a less significant role these days. The intention until the turn of the millennium was to cater only to well heeled visitors with luxury accommodation, but with the chronic shortage of foreign currency the current government has decided to promote private initiatives such as guesthouses and holiday apartment. While the Seychelles is still is not a cheap travel destination, an affordable holiday in one of the numerous guesthouses is quite possible. Per year there are only about 200,000 visitors to the islands, the majority of them from Europe.

The Vallée de Mai nature reserve on Praslin is one of the two World Heritage Sites on the Seychelles and when you stroll through it you will be inspired enough to think that God must have had a creative day when He scattered these islands off the African coast in the Indian Ocean. None are alike and each has something special to discover.

1970 The Seychelles have their own constitution

1976 The islands gain their independence and James R. Mancham (SDP) becomes the first President

1977 France Albert René (SPUP) ousts Mancham in a coup and is declared the new President

1993 René wins in the first multi-party elections in 16 years

2004 James A. Michel replaces France Albert René and is re-elected in 2006 and 2011

Cruising the islands by boat makes island-hopping twice the fun

The islands are lush and fertile and if you come from the other side of the equator, you will be impressed by the myriad of shapes, colours, scale and the density of the vegetation. But the nature on the islands is not particularly species-rich and not all of it is indigenous anymore. The indigenous forest around the edge of the islands was cleared and – with the exception of a few places – the original vegetation was replaced with new plants.

Giant tortoises and coco de mer

However, you still find plants and animals that occur nowhere else in the world and there are legions of botanists and ornithologists working to preserve the wildlife that is indigenous to the Seychelles and trying to restore the environment. The legendary coco de mer – the palm nut that has inspired so many myths – is one of the 80 plants endemic to the Seychelles. Another unique speciality are the giant tortoises, the 'living fossils' of a bygone era. At one point they were near extinction but there are now more than 170,000 specimens on the islands. Also under protection are 13 bird species that only live on the Seychelles, such as the small Brown Noddy, the mighty Frigatebird and the Red-tailed Tropicbird. Like almost all the planet's coral reefs, those of the Seychelles were also affected by the El Niño climate phenomenon. Nevertheless, the country's natural attractions – especially the marine flora and fauna, which has recovered in many places – is still the country's real drawcard and the raison d'être for its tourism trade. As a result the government has placed about half of the total land area and parts of its coastline under protection and some of the islands are only open to botanists and ornithologists with tourists only allowed access under exceptional circumstances.

WHAT'S HOT

1 Dear to the heart

Jewellery These souvenirs are both beautiful and long lasting! The creative minds of *Kreolor (Camion Hall, Albert Street, Victoria, Mahé, www.kreolorseychelles.com, photo)* craft unique necklaces and rings, combs and bangles out of coconut, shells, wood and seeds. The jewellery and craft items reflect old traditions but are also quite modern: pieces made from natural materials, such as metal and stones or colourful fabrics that are ideal for city life.

2 Island inspiration

Art Swaying palms and splashing water – the island is both home to and inspiration for artist George Camille. In his studio *(Kaz Zanana, Revolution Avenue, Victoria, Mahé)* you can watch him while he works. Andrew Gee welcomes visitors to view his works, inspired by the Seychelles, in his studio *(Baie Lazare, Mahé)*, while sculptor, Tom Bowers, *(Santa Maria Estate, Anse à la Mouche, Mahé, photo)* creates works whose theme are the beauty of the island.

3 Beautiful fragrances

Island fragrances The Seychelles are a dream for the olfactory senses and the locals have set about capturing their heady scents in little bottles. One such enterprise is *Kreolfleurage (North East Point, Mahé, photo)*, where the scent of the island is captured in a blend of hibiscus, elephant grass and takamaka resin. You can buy it at *SenP (Camion Hall, Albert Street, Victoria, Mahé)*, at the *Pineapple Studio (Anse aux Poules Bleues)* or on site, where you can also have a guided tour of the facility. At the *Bonjour* perfumery *(Victoria Estate Building, Victoria, Mahé)* there are no secrets: you can experience the contents of the perfume yourself.

There are a lot of things to discover on the Seychelles. Here is our hand-picked selection

Jump in

4

Sporty Diving, sailing, snorkelling – these are the usual activities on the Seychelles but there are also other sports on offer. What only a few people know is that the wind blows off the Seychelles and the perfect surfing and windsurfing months are from June to September. The professionals from *Tropicsurf (www.tropicsurf.net)* know where a breeze is currently blowing on the private island Frégate. The company specialises in luxury surf trips that include candlelight dinners on the beach and excellent wines and accommodation. Even if the wind is not blowing, you can still get on to the water: with stand up paddle board surfing you don't need any wind, but you do need a long paddle *(c/o Four Seasons, Petite Anse, Mahé)*. Another option is to explore the dive world a little faster with a sea scooter. This environmentally-friendly machine is an ideal (and fast) way for divers and snorkellers to get from one dive site to the next *(c/o Angel Fish Dive Operations, Roche Caiman, Mahé)*.

From the garden

5

... to the table The produce on your plate at *La Plaine St André (Mahé)* is absolutely fresh as it is sourced from their own garden, and the ingredients used at *North Island Resorts (Mahé, photo)* are just as fresh, as they too grow their own produce in their garden. *Maria's Rock Café (Baie Lazare, Mahé)* is in an unusual location, tucked away in a cave; they prepare the fish dishes at your table on hot lava stones and serve them with vegetable side dishes. The latter often harvested by Maria Soubana herself such as the local chilli variety the *pimente kabrí*, which flourish in Soubana's mother's garden.

IN A NUTSHELL

CLIMATE

The Seychelles has a tropical climate with consistent temperatures throughout the year. The average temperature is 26.6°C/80°F and it seldom gets hotter than 32°C/90°F. The months of May to October are pleasant and dry but there can be strong southeastly monsoon rains. December to March is hotter and more humid and the monsoon comes from the north-west. However, given the large expanse of the archipelago, the climatic conditions do vary depending on the region. The water temperature is stable throughout the year at 26–30°C/80–85°F and the sun shines on average for 6–8 hours a day. Mean relative humidity is around 75% with cooling breezes.

COCO DE MER

A botanical rarity, the ● *coco de mer*, is unique to the Seychelles and grows only on Praslin and Curieuse (a few specimens are also in the Botanical Gardens in Victoria). The coco de mer got its name even before the discovery of the Seychelles. The nuts were carried on the ocean currents and deposited on distant shores where they were thought to be the fruit of a huge underwater tree. Everything about the coco de mer is large: the seed from which it grows is considered the

Photo: A group of hikers in the Morne Seychellois National Park

A blaze of colour and joie de vivre: sun-drenched islands where the world is still a wonderful place

largest in the botanical world, the trunk makes its way up through even the densest of forests, and the nut itself weighs a good 20kg/45lbs. The leaves have a wide surface and their stems are long so that they can compete against other plants for sparse sunlight. The manner in which the coco de mer propagates also has a local legend. The male plant has a phallus-like extension, the matching counterpart can be found in the fruit of the female plant. On stormy nights, according to the Seychellois, the male trees uproot themselves and approach the female trees to reproduce, a process that no one has managed to capture yet. While the pollination is still not fully understood, botanists have a far more profane explanation: the ripe nuts fall to the ground, and after about one year a seedling takes roots and over the course of many years it becomes a tree. It takes a quarter of a century for the young tree to bear its first fruit. Its life expectancy is about 200 to 400 years. For centuries the coco de mer nut was considered a symbol of wealth and prosperity. Today it is a popular, if somewhat large souvenir from the Seychelles; about 2000 are sold to tourists each year.

CREOLE

Creole developed in the overseas territories of European colonial powers, where the local languages and dialects mixed with the language of the colonizers. The Creole spoken on the Seychelles is *Seselwa* and is based on French phonetics and syntax. Today it is an official language and is used in schools as the official language of instruction.

ECONOMY

The most important industry in the economy is tourism, which brings in over 70 per cent of the foreign exchange revenue and about a third of the gross national product. Other significant contributors are fishing and the production of copra, the main export product until a few decades ago. Dried coconut is used as a raw material in the chemical industry and is used in the production of soap, shampoo, detergent, candles and synthetic resin varnish. The coconut plantations occupy most of the utilised agricultural area and provide the majority of the population with work. Industry exists only on a modest scale, but the government is seeking new sites on Mahé for the establishment of manufacturing companies. The most important export commodities

Rare species: White Terns on Bird Island

include frozen and canned fish, copra and spices such as cinnamon and vanilla.

ESMERALDA & CO.

Nowhere else in the world are there as many giant tortoises as on the Seychelles. The largest and oldest among them is Esmeralda who, despite the name, is actually a male. He weighs in at about 298kg/560lbs and is believed to be about 120–150 years old. These sedate creatures are relics of a past epoch and were culled to the point of extinction, because when the first seafarers arrived at the Seychelles, these creatures served as a practical source of meat and when the ships set sail again they frequently took dozens of live tortoises on board, which were then slaughtered for fresh meat during the course of the voyage. The result was a drastic depletion of the species. The end to the slaughtering of these animals was first brought about when the government introduced a protection measure and then by the international condemnation of the enjoyment of tortoise meat, specifically tortoise soup. In addition, access to their nesting and breeding sites was also restricted. Since then the number of tortoises has grown significantly and today there are an estimated 170,000 giant tortoises on the Seychelles. Most of the animals live on the Aldabra Atoll, but they can also be found on almost all of the other islands in the Seychelles.

FAUNA

On Bird Island you won't only get to know Esmeralda, but also – as with the other islands – many exotic birds such as the *Sooty* and *White Tern*. On La Digue you can see the rare *Paradise Flycatcher*, on the Aldabra Atoll the *White-throated Rail* and the *Aldabra Drongo*, a songbird. There are also countless species of seagulls, swallows and other birds that are typical of the tropics, such as the *White-tailed* and *Red-tailed Tropicbird*. The *Great Frigatebird* are the most powerful seabirds, with a wingspan of up to 2m/6.5ft, while on the island of Frégate there is a zoological rarity, the *Seychelles Magpie Robin*. Destruction of their habitat put them on the brink of extinction only a few years ago but, due to preservation efforts, there are now about 80 specimens of this inconspicuous black and white bird. Some interesting *lizards, salamanders* and *geckos* also reside here. The latter are particularly popular because they like to eat vermin.

FLORA

There was once a time when almost all the islands were covered with dense tropical forest. Today the vegetation is shaped by mankind but this has made little dent in the country's natural splendour. The largest diversity can be found on the main island of Mahé but it is also here where you will find visible traces of man's careless treatment of nature: where mangroves and hardwood forests once stretched out, there are now secondary forests with low species diversity and alien vegetation. They consist mostly of coconut palms and the imported species of *Eucalyptus* and *Albizzia,* as well as ornamental plants like such as *hibiscus* and *bougainvillea*. The indigenous forests are now only found in the higher elevations. In the Seychelles there are many plants that cannot be found – or found only in small numbers – anywhere else in the world. Some of them were not always indigenous; many species were brought in as seeds or seedlings from other islands and some are botanical rarities, such as the *bwa-d-fer* (Ironwood tree), with only a few surviving, or the *Jellyfish* tree, whose flowers look like an upside down jelly fish.

Also only found in the Seychelles is the aromatic *Seychelles Vanilla Orchid* with its large, white flowers. There are countless palm trees, one of which provides *palm of hearts*, a vegetable harvested from the core and tips of the palm and is used to make the exquisite 'Millionaire's Salad'. The country's two most economically important trees are the coconut tree – they are processed from root to palm leaf – and *cinnamon tree*, which was introduced from Ceylon (now Sri Lanka) in 1772 by the French Governor Pierre Poivre. The smooth, aromatic bark of the tree is either ground into a spice or stripped and dried into small, curled sticks. Whilst its cultivation was for many years unprofitable, today it is a thriving industry. Further important spice plants are *clove, vanilla, citronella* and *patchouli*.

A chat in Creole

GEOGRAPHY

The Seychelles archipelago Economic Exclusive Zone extends over a surface area of more 385,000mi² but of that the actual land area is 175mi². Topographically the Seychelles belong to the African continent; the Inner Islands are the scattered remnants from the geologically ancient super-continent of Gondwana. The Inner Islands with an area of about 12,000mi² includes 32 islands, almost all of which are granite. The Outer Islands area covers about 155,000mi² and these islands are primarily reef islets and low-lying coral islands such as the Amirante and the Aldabra Atoll. The distance between the main island of Mahé and the African mainland is about 1600km/1000mi.

NATIONAL PARKS

The islands of Aride, Cousin and Curieuse as well as Morne Seychellois National Park on Mahé are all protected national parks and reserves. The Vallée de Mai on Praslin and the Aldabra Atoll are both World Heritage Sites and parts of the ocean surrounding the islands also fall under protected areas. Bathing is allowed in these protected areas on condition that swimmers show respect for nature. The following are two of the most interesting Marine National Parks: *Baie Ternay* at the westernmost tip of Mahé is a narrow bay only accessible by boat. Damaged in the past by divers the coral reef is now slowly regenerating. It has a rich marine life and some diverse sea grass (e.g. *Turbinia*) and it is the spawning ground for hawksbill turtles.

The *Curieuse National Park* is off the coast of Praslin; the reserve covers 3650 acres of which four-fifths is land and one-fifth water. The park includes the island of Curieuse as well as the channel which separates the island from the Anse Boudin. Some of the island's protected species include hawksbill turtles, giant tortoises, the iconic coco de mers as well as the mangrove forests of Turtle Bay.

POLITICS

One might think that the Seychellois live in paradise: free education until university level, free medical and hospital treatments, a state guaranteed pension and other social services. For the local population these are the positive consequences of a government that ran for decades along Socialist lines. The introduction of these benefits was only possible with the energetic support of other Socialist governments, such as the former Soviet Union and East Germany. This massive development aid made the Seychelles – in comparison to its neighbours on the African continent – a prosperous welfare state that was soon able to realize dreams that were nearly impossible in other countries.

With the demise of the Soviet Union and the dissolution of East Germany came the end of the aid subsidies, and any increase in the revenue from tourism could hardly offset the loss of income. The result was a new policy, in which the former head of government France Albert René was forced to agree to privatisation, which gave the government control again of the economy. But this brought only partial success and in the mid 1990s the Seychelles experienced an acute shortage of foreign exchange. René's successor, James Alix Michel, facilitated foreign business ventures and set up a free port, which made the Seychelles into a hub for the trade in goods. And lastly, the government granted permission for the construction of new hotels and guest accommodation which could also be run by private individuals in the form of guesthouses. It is now also the government's declared aim to encourage the tourism sector to become more environmentally friendly and to practice sustainable tourism through conservation.

POPULATION

About 87,500 Seychellois, in Creole *Seselwa*, live on the 115 or so islands that make up the Republic of the Seychelles. There is no indigenous population and the Seychellois are a diverse ethnic mix of immigrants. The population is concentrated on the two islands of Mahé and Praslin – and a few smaller islands in the surrounding area – where close to 90 per cent of the population lives. The population density is the greatest on Mahé. The Seychelles has a very young population: almost a quarter of the inhabitants are currently under the age of 14 years and the average age is about 28 years.

RELIGION

Almost 90 per cent of the population are Catholic and going to mass on Sundays plays a major role in the lives of most Seychellois. However, many Seychellois secretly maintain their beliefs in superstitions, mysticism and witchcraft – similar to the West African voodoo cults – a syncretism that is typical for former slave areas. The seers or *bonom di bwa* are called upon when, for example, someone wants to find out why a partner is behaving strangely, or why someone has died a sudden death.

FOOD & DRINK

The term 'Creole cuisine' is strictly speaking not precise enough for that which is boiled, grilled and baked in Seychellois pots, pans and ovens. It is far better speak of it as 'Seychelles cuisine', one that – inspired by the ethnic diversity of the locals – is a blend of various other national cuisines.

Each demographic group has contributed different elements from their own cooking so there are Asian, Indian and African as well as European dishes that form part of the local cuisine. The latter are the remnants of the colonial era. The Seychellois rarely season with strong spices, more often than not they make use of a combination of fragrant spices such as turmeric, cloves, cinnamon, ginger, garlic, mint, pepper, cardamom and nutmeg. The careful combination determines whether or not the dish's main ingredient has a taste of its own or is overpowered by spices. Another strong influence from Indian cuisine are the curries, of which there are a wide variety of dishes, each one of them distinguished by their own individual flavour. Popular favourites are vegetable curries, where different types of vegetables are cut into small pieces, cooked in a pot and seasoned with the aforementioned blend of curry spices. Delicious fish (such as Bonito) curries are also often on the

Photo: Chicken with rice and vegetables

The Seychelles cuisine is fresh, down to earth and characterised by rice and fish dishes, but it also offers some delicious surprises

menu and if a curry is too hot, it is softened with coconut milk.

The main courses are generally fish, chicken or beef. Fish is cheap; it is caught all around the islands and usually sold on the same day. But there are also some differences and certain fish, such as Bonito (part of the tuna family) are considered a poor man's fish. Others are more expensive (and therefore a treat for the locals) such as swordfish, octopus and mackerel, which you can find on almost every restaurant menu. A typical Seychelles speciality is *bourzwa* or Red Snapper. It is usually served whole and due to its size is enough for the whole table. The swordfish is also deliciousand is usually served as a thick, grilled steak. Some of the special delicacies are lobster, crab and crayfish, they are usually served grilled.

LOCAL SPECIALITIES

- **bouyon bred** – cabbage soup seasoned with spices such as garlic, ginger and pepper
- **kari pwason** – a variety of different fish are used to make this fish curry, which has a slightly sour taste from the tamarinds
- **kari zourit** – creamy octopus curry, which is prepared with fresh coconut milk and cinnamon leaves
- **ladob banann** – popular dessert of bananas cooked with sugar, salt and vanilla in coconut milk
- **lasos kreol** – Creole sauce made from tomatoes, onions, bilimbi fruit, garlic, ginger and chilli and used as a fish marinade or sauce
- **lasoup pwason** – soup made of tender, white fish fried with onion in oil and then simmered with spices
- **lasoup tektek** – mussel soup made from tiny white mussels that are collected on the beach, often prepared with pumpkin
- **pwason griye** – grilled fish (e.g. tuna) that has first been marinated in garlic, ginger, onions and peppers and served with rice and a spicy Creole sauce
- **pwason sale** – salted, dried (and therefore preserved) fish that is usually offered during the seasons when the fish are scarce (during the south-east monsoons)
- **satini** – all dishes go well with these spicy chutneys made of local fruits such as mango, papaya and coconuts
- **stek ton** – fresh tuna fish, first marinated in Creole sauce and then grilled or baked

A meal often begins with a soup (called *bouyon* regardless of the ingredients). Among the starters the 'Millionaire's Salad' comes out tops, deserving of its name. The salad is made with heart of palms, in order to get to the edible heart of the palm you need to cut down the whole palm. As this is prohibited, they have to wait until a palm falls by itself and since this rarely happens – much to the chagrin of gourmets – the price is very high. In restaurants rice is served with every meal, sometimes there also potatoes, mostly in the form of fried chips. The locals prefer manioc, sweet potatoes, breadfruit or green bananas as a side dish.

An expensive dessert delicacy is the very sweet jelly-like flesh of the green *coco de mer*. For the average citizen there are also affordable fruits cooked in a sweet coconut milk sauce called *daubes*. And of course there are bananas – the smaller they are, the sweeter they taste. Passion fruit, avocado, papaya and oranges are offered fresh at the market in Victoria along with the all important coconut, which provides not only a refreshing sap but also some delicious white flesh.

Also among the drinks on the islands is a local speciality, the *calou*. This is the half-fermented sap of unripe coconuts, which has a slightly intoxicating effect. Although there are alcoholic drinks, they are imported which makes them quite expensive. One exception is the *Seybrew* beer, which is brewed near Victoria, according to German purity standards.

Each hotel in the Seychelles operates at least one restaurant, but non-guests are welcome almost everywhere. But if you only dine in the hotel restaurants you will be missing out on one of the greatest holiday pleasures. There are a whole range of speciality restaurants on Mahé, Praslin and La Digue, which serve the most delectable Creole dishes. Recommended restaurants are found in the main chapters of this travel guide in the 'Food & Drink' section.

In the Seychelles you will search in vain if you are looking for McDonald's or any other fast food chains, this (supposed) gap is filled by several small ● takeaway restaurants, mainly in the capital Victoria. There is very good Creole fare to take away, for example every day from 11 o'clock you can get delicious *samosas*, pastries fried filled with spicy vegetables, meat and chicken. One portion is enough for two and only costs about 30 rupees.

Dinner is served

SHOPPING

Most of the souvenirs shops are in the centre of Victoria, the capital of the Seychelles, where there are a number of small wooden huts displaying local arts and crafts. However, the prices here are inflated and bargaining is seldom an option. It is also worth taking a closer look at the items as many of the goods are not from the Seychelles; look out for 'Made in China' tags. For normal purchases a good option is *Ocean Gate House* which has a number of shops and a few small galleries, it is situated towards the lower end of Independence Avenue. *Makishop*, a shop at the upper end of Beau Vallon on Mahé, has some good quality tee shirts and casual wear with imaginative Seychelles designs.

ARTS & CRAFTS

Pottery, both artistic as well as plain, and batik work can be found in the handicraft village *Vilaz Artizanal* on the road between Victoria and Anse Royale, 14km/8.5mi outside from Victoria. Local artisans display their products in small huts *(see p. 48)*. A good opportunity to purchase local arts and crafts is also at the various *culture bazaars*, which takes place every month at different locations on Mahé (information at the Seychelles Tourist Board in Victoria). At *Kenwyn House* on Francis Rachel Street in Victoria *(tel. 422 44 40)* there are not only handicraft souvenirs, but also fine jewellery.

COCO DE MER

Probably the most unusual souvenir (and the heaviest) from the Seychelles is the *coco de mer* (known locally as *koko dmer)*. On average 2000 of these nuts are annually processed into souvenirs; only those with an official certificate may be exported as the palm trees are a protected species. You can get a coco de mer at a reasonable price at the Botanical Garden on Mahé, but you can expect to pay a very hefty price of between 2600 to 5200 rupees. A word of warning: if you try to export a coco de mer without a certificate, you will be issued with a steep fine, not only when leaving the Seychelles, but also when entering Europe and the coco de mer will also be confiscated.

Model boats and coconuts: only a few souvenirs originate in the Seychelles, but despite this there are plenty of novel gifts

MODEL BOATS

A souvenir that is not entirely cheap is a true to scale model boat. It is cheaper to buy them at the workshops (rather than in the souvenir shops) and you also get to see just how time-consuming it is to produce a model, such as the 'Santa Maria' from Christopher Columbus' fleet. The model builders from *La Marine Model Ships* in La Plaine St André on Mahé *(Mon–Fri 9am–4pm)* are famed for their craft. A good place to go is also the *Souverains des Mers* boutique in Le Rocher *(5km/3mi south of Victoria)* with a permanent choice of about 40 models. If you purchase a model boat, you should insist on good packaging!

STAMPS

The colourful Seychelles postage stamps are carefully crafted with exotic, detailed designs that make them a firm favourite with collectors from all over the world and represent an important source of income for the local post office. The first day covers – as well as individual stamps and complete sets – are highly prized and can be bought at the issue price at a special counter at the main post office in Victoria. You can also take out a subscription for future issues, the stamps are then sent to you on a regular basis.

TEA & SPICES

Vanilla, cinnamon and other spices from the Seychelles are the most inexpensive at the market in Victoria *(see p. 37)* but they are also available in grocery stores on the other islands. You can also purchase Seychelles tea there, but the choice is somewhat limited.

THE PERFECT ROUTE

MAHÉ – THE SMALLEST CAPITAL IN THE WORLD

The first day is dedicated to the main island of Mahé. A good point of departure for a tour is the centre of 1 *Victoria* → p. 33. Start with an early morning visit (8am at the very latest) to the *Sir Selwyn Selwyn Clarke Market.* A stroll through the market does not take long, but it will give you a good impression of the islanders' way of life. If you have a car, take the road leading south from Mahé and go past Mont Fleuri and the airport and after about 12km/7.5mi you reach 2 *Anse Royale* → p. 89 (photo left). You should make a few stops on the way – some places have magnificent views of the south-east coast and the ocean. Is it already midday? Then it is time for a light snack or a pizza at *Kaz Kreol*. It is lovely to sit out on their terrace right on the beach. You now cross the island to *Anse à la Mouche.* The journey continues to the north via Anse Boileau and Grand' Anse to Port Glaud, where you turn right and drive on winding roads through the hinterland towards Victoria. At the entrance the road leads to the left to the 3 *Beau Vallon Bay* → p. 44, the liveliest beach on Mahé. If you continue driving, you will reach the northernmost point, 4 *North Point* → p. 44. From here it is only a short drive back to Victoria where you can end the day with a delicious dinner at *Marie Antoinette.*

ISLAND HOPPING

On the second day you also have to have an early start: the plane to 5 *Praslin* → p. 60 leaves at 8.15am, the flight is just 15 minutes. It is worthwhile renting a car for the island and you can book one on Mahé. From the airport, which is situated on the southern side of the island, you continue in a southerly direction and after about 5km/3mi you take a left turn and after a further 3km/1.8mi you will reach the World Heritage Site 6 *Vallée de Mai* → p. 63. Allow about two hours for a walk through this amazing valley with its unbelievable diversity of plants, including many specimens of the legendary coco de mer. Then it continues back down towards the sea to the harbour of Praslin at the *Baie Ste Anne.* After turning left twice, you will reach *Anse Volbert.* Here on one of the most beautiful beaches on Praslin – with

Experience the diverse facets of the beautiful Seychelles with trips on the main island of Mahé, Praslin and La Digue

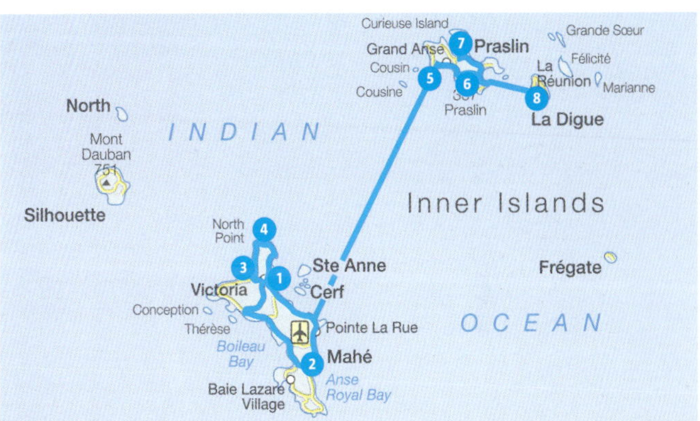

crystal clear water and soft sand – you should allow yourself some time for a break. Afterwards you can continue your drive along Anse Volbert and then turn into the *La Goulue* cafeteria where there are not only Creole snacks at affordable prices but also wonderful views of the beautiful bay. Not far from here is *Anse Petite Cour* and 7 ***Anse Possession*** → p. 62, where Marion Dufresne erected the Possession Stone in 1768; you can stay over at the *La Reserve* hotel or in the new *Raffles Praslin*, one of the best addresses in Praslin.

POSTCARD IMAGE ON LA DIGUE

Not to see 8 ***La Digue*** → p. 57 (photo middle) is not to have seen the Seychelles. It is instantly recognisable from postcards with images such as the towering, ancient granite boulders at the *Pointe Source d'Argent*. As there is no airport in La Digue, take the passenger schooner which travels twice daily from Praslin and then hire a bicycle when you land on the island. Just set out on your bike, the road is well built and you can't miss the sign to the famous granite rocks. Also nearby is the *L'Union Estate* coconut plantation, where you can observe the processing of coconuts. So as not to end the day on a stressful note, it is advisable to stay overnight on La Digue, for example at the *La Digue Island Lodge* or at the less expensive *Patatran Village*. The next morning you can return to Praslin on the passenger schooner and from there take a plane back to Mahé.

Surface distance: approx. 100km/62mi
Recommended travel time: three days
Detailed map of the route on the back cover, in the road atlas and the pull-out map

MAHÉ

With an area of 60 square miles, Mahé is by far the largest island in the Seychelles – and also the most densely populated. Its length in the north-south direction is 27km/16.5mi, its widest point is only 8km/5mi. Mahé is usually the first point of contact for all visitors, because the only international airport is located here.

Like most of the islands in the Seychelles, Mahé is also a granite island. Its highest summit ✻ *Morne Seychellois* is situated in the northern part of the island, south of Victoria, and reaches an impressive 905m/2969ft. Other outstanding topographic features are the summits of *Trois Frères* (699m/2293ft), *Morne Blanc* (667m/2188ft) and *Mount Harrison* (688m/2257ft). These lofty peaks are often covered in thick mist. The west is more fragmented and more mountainous than the flatter east. The most beautiful beaches on Mahé can be found on the west coast: *Grand' Anse,* the *Anse à la Mouche* and the *Baie Lazare.* Between the capital Victoria and the international airport an entire coral lagoon was drained out for the 1993 Indian Ocean Games. Modern sports venues and housing developments were built on the site.

Since the interior of the island is difficult to build on, land on the east coast was

Photo: Anse Intendance, Mahé

Palm trees, beguiling beaches and a peaceful capital: when you arrive, you might find your own little paradise on earth right here

reclaimed with landfills the east coast in the years before the turn of the century. Now known as *Eden Island*, it was developed as an exclusive residential marina by a South African investor and there are now 450 luxury houses and apartments for wealthy Seychellois and foreigners. The artificial island with lagoons and piers is connected to the mainland by a causeway *(www.edenisland.sc)*.

VICTORIA

MAP INSIDE BACK COVER
(116 B–C 5–6) *(D–E10)* **According to reliable sources, Victoria is the smallest capital in the world, what is certain is that it is the only city in the Seychelles. Its layout makes it hard to distinguish its boundaries, as there is a**

Victoria: view from Bel Air over the harbour to the outlying islands

smooth transition from the centre to the surrounding suburbs.

Victoria is divided into six districts: Bel Air, a part of English River, Mont Fleuri, Mount Buxton, Plaisance and St Louis. About 23,000 people live here – that is slightly more than a third of the total population of the Seychelles. Victoria is of course the seat of the government, houses all the authorities and is thus placed in the centre of public life. The latter takes place mostly on weekdays – on Sundays the little city is usually very quiet and deserted.

The chic suburb of Victoria is *Bel Air* where there are some magnificent views of Victoria, the harbour area and the outlying islands. From here it is only a few miles on the Sans Souci road to reach *Sans Souci,* where the houses become fewer and the forest denser. The Cypriot Archbishop Makarios took a villa here, a short distance away from the road, as his home in 1956, after he was forced to leave the Mediterranean island for political reasons.

> CITY **WHERE TO START?**
> **Clock Tower:** the landmark on the intersection of Independence Avenue, Albert Street and Francis Rachel Street is the meeting point for the capital Victoria. There are shops, banks, agencies, the main post office and the National Museum in the area. Independence Ave leads via Freedom Square, and the Bicentennial Monument, to the harbour.

SIGHTSEEING

BOTANICAL GARDENS 

Founded in 1771, the Botanical Gardens have at least one specimen of all the botanical rarities that grow on the Seychelles.

Right at the entrance you can see to the left and right of the path the only *coco de mer* trees growing outside the islands of La Digue, Praslin and Curieuse. The upper part of the park has largely been left in its natural state. There is also a small restaurant, *Le Sapin.* The Botanical Gardens are not only there for leisure activities, there are also various research facilities where scientific experiments with plants are carried out. *Above Mont Fleuri Road | daily 8am–5pm | admission 100 rupees*

CATHEDRAL OF THE IMMACULATE CONCEPTION

If you continue from the market on Church Street in a northerly direction, you will come to the Cathedral of the Immaculate Conception, consecrated in 1874, the largest church in the Seychelles. On Sundays the children born in wedlock are baptised here – on Fridays, those out of wedlock. Since three quarters of the babies in the Seychelles are born out of wedlock, the priests have their hands full on Fridays. The bells of the corresponding towers reached a certain literary fame. In his novel 'Where the Clock Chimes Twice', the English writer Alec Waugh mentions the peculiarity of chiming twice on the hour: once at the right time and the second time for the daydreamers and slowcoaches two minutes later *(mass: Mon–Fri 6am, Sat 5pm, Sun 7am and 9am).* Also noteworthy is the imposing two-storey building next to the cathedral, called *La Domus.* It was built out of granite rock in 1934 by Swiss missionaries and today still serves as a residence for Roman Catholic clerics and monks.

MONUMENTS

On the roundabout where Independence and 5th June Avenues meet, is a modern sculpture, the *Bicentennial Monument.* It is a symbol of the African, Asian and European continents – where most of the Seychellois come from. Also noteworthy is the *Zonn Lib*, the stylized statue of

MARCO POLO HIGHLIGHTS

★ Bel Air
From here you have spectacular views of Victoria and the harbour area → p. 34

★ Botanical Gardens
One of the oldest in the world → p. 34

★ Bel Air Cemetery
In search of Louis XVII → p. 36

★ Cerf Island
Island paradise near Victoria → p. 42

★ Anse Soleil Café
Creole cuisine at its best and a great location right on the beach → p. 38

★ Sir Selwyn Selwyn Clarke Market
Victoria's meeting place for locals and holidaymakers → p. 37

★ National Museum
History brought to life: a visit won't take long, but will leave a lasting impression → p. 36

★ Hiking on Mahé
Trails vary in difficulty, from easy to average → p. 40

★ La Scala
The location of the restaurant is breathtaking, the cuisine delicious → p. 45

★ Anse Intendance
The sea here can be wild with huge waves crashing down on this beautiful beach → p. 47

a man who holds the broken chains of slavery in his hands *(on 5th June Avenue)*. The statue was created by a local artist on the occasion of the Seychelles' Declaration of Independence; it was inaugurated in 1978 and dedicated to the martyrs who rebelled against colonisation and oppression on 5 June 1977.

BEL AIR CEMETERY ★

From Revolution Avenue head south and then turn into Bel Air Road and after a short walk you be in the suburb of Bel Air. On the left hand side lies the Bel Air Cemetery which was restored a few years ago. Unfortunately the inscriptions on the weathered tombstones are quite hard to decipher. It is said there are some pirates' graves here. Perhaps you will find Louis Poiret's grave, he claimed to be the legitimate son of the deposed Louis XVI and therefore the lost King of France, a claim since refuted by scientists through genetic tests.

GRAND TRIANON

This colonial style house on Revolution Avenue once housed a famous guest: in his search for his colleague David Livingstone, the British explorer of Africa, Henry Morton Stanley, made this a stopover (1841–1904). Today the building houses the *Marie Antoinette* restaurant *(see 'Food & Drink')*.

ARUL MIHU NAVASAKTHI VINAYAGAR HINDU TEMPLE ●

The only Hindu temple in the Seychelles is not far from the centre of Victoria. The ornate and colourful temple was built in 1992 and named after Vinayagar, the god of safety and prosperity. It is worth paying attention to the gate tower that is richly decorated with Hindu deities, called Gopuram. *Quincy Street | daily 6am–midday and 5pm–9pm | admission free*

INSIDER TIP KENWYN HOUSE ●

If you are interested in Seychelles art, you will definitely find something here. Kenwyn House, a historic wooden building, offers an art gallery, where works by artists living in the Seychelles are exhibited. The building itself is an exceptional example of 19th century colonial architecture and served for many years as the seat for the telephone company Cable & Wireless, before it was converted into an exclusive souvenir shop. There is also an art exhibition of paintings and needless to say the works of Sir Michael Adams, the 'Gauguin of the Seychelles' are also on display. The works by other artists such as George Camille and Barbara Jenson are just as colourful and vibrant. One floor is reserved for a South African jewellery retailer and the valuable items (pearls, diamonds) are exempt from VAT. *Francis Rachel Street | Mon–Fri 9am–5pm, Sat 9am–1pm | admission free | www.kenwynhouse.com*

NATIONAL LIBRARY BUILDING/ NATIONAL ARCHIVES ●

Those interested in the history, geography and literature of the Seychelles, will find lots of interesting information here. Since 1995 the surprisingly rich national archive has been located in this modern glass and steel building not far from the centre of Victoria. The reading room is pleasantly air-conditioned and the staff are happy to inform visitors on specific topics. *Francis Rachel Street | Mon–Fri 8.30am–3.30pm, Sat 8.30am–midday | admission free*

NATIONAL MUSEUM ★ ●

Just behind the Clock Tower on Francis Rachel Street lies the National Museum of the Seychelles. It provides a good insight into the history of the archipelago. On display are documents and historical nautical charts, weapons and cannons, model boats and traditional musical instruments. You can also find the *Possession Stone* here that was laid by Captain Nicolas Morphey in 1756. Temporary art exhibitions also regularly take place in the National Museum. *State House Avenue | Mon/Tue, Thu/Fri 8.30am–4.30pm, Wed 8.30am–midday, Sat 9am–1pm | admission 15 rupees*

SIR SELWYN SELWYN CLARKE MARKET ★ ●

If you visit Victoria on a Saturday morning, it is worth your while to take a stroll through the *Sir Selwyn Selwyn Clarke Market*. It is slightly set back on Albert Street, only a short walk from the Clock Tower. In order to experience it in all its diversity, you should get up as early as the Seychellois. They start arriving there at 6am to do their weekend shopping because that is when the best variety is on offer; it is also fun to browse in the shops around the market. Perhaps you will find a pretty souvenir or gift for those back home in the motley mix of goods on offer. It is best to have plenty of coins on hand as most of the traders don't have change for larger denominations. *Albert Street*

CITY CENTRE

To dispel a common misconception: the *Clock Tower*, a prominent orientation point near the end of Independence Avenue, is not a miniature version of Big Ben, but of the clock tower at Vauxhall Bridge in London. It was a gift from the British government, erected in 1903, when the Seychelles took the first step towards independence. There is a lot of activity on weekdays around the clock tower. Not far from there are several wooden houses with souvenir vendors selling arts and crafts made in the Seychelles, as well as a large number of other shops, boutiques, banks and travel agencies. The main post

The market in Victoria has the best produce on offer in the early morning

office is also found here. If you turn left into Francis Rachel Street, you will see the pretty, INSIDER TIP colourful colonial style wooden houses.

ST PAUL'S CATHEDRAL

On 14 May 1859 the first Anglican Bishop of Mauritius, Vincent William Ryan, consecrated the cathedral on Revolution Avenue, which is the Anglican parish church of Victoria. In 1920, when the British abolished the entire government of Mauritius and the Seychelles, it became the Bishop's official secondary residence. Its modern appearance is as a result of alterations and extensions done between 2001 and 2004. Today it can accommodate about 800 worshippers. *Mass: Mon midday, Tue 6.30am, Wed 9am, Thu 5.30am, Fri 6.30am and midday, Sat 5pm and Sun 6.30am and 8.30am*

LOW BUDGET

▶ Set in pretty surrounding *Les Manguiers* guesthouse only has three rooms, about 15 minutes by car from Victoria. 1200 rupees per night per room, self-catering, kitchen available. No air-conditioning! *Machabée | Mahé | tel. 424 14 55*

▶ Every Wednesday from 5pm there is a small bazaar at the *Coral Strand Hotel*, where you can experience not only local art and music by candlelight, but where you can also buy some pretty and affordably priced souvenirs.

▶ Longing for Italian cuisine? Then you should head to the *Baobab Pizzeria* at the end of Beau Vallon Beach. The wood oven pizzas start from 39 rupees, the restaurant is situated right on the beach. *Daily | tel. 424 71 67*

▶ Under no circumstances should you miss out the underwater world of the Seychelles and ● the *Underwater Centre* offers reasonably priced trial diving courses. *Tel 434 54 45 | www.diveseychelles.com*

FOOD & DRINK

ANSE SOLEIL CAFÉ ★

Situated right on the beach at Anse Soleil, south of Victoria. Open for lunch (and on request also in the evenings) serving delicious Creole cuisine. You will not go hungry. *Daily midday–8pm | Anse Soleil | tel. 436 10 85 | Budget–Moderate*

BEL AIR

You need to make a timely reservation because this restaurant only has a few tables. It belongs to the Hotel Bel Air hotel and was completely renovated in 2012. There is no menu as the service is a buffet. The flavours are all uniquely Creole, the ingredients very fresh as the chef shops daily at the market. *Only for lunch, closed Sun | Bel Air Road | tel. 422 44 16 | Budget*

DOUBLECLICK SEYCHELLES

As the name suggests, you can not only eat and drink here but also surf the Internet or check your emails. The menu includes simple, inexpensive dishes and some international snacks. The wonderful view of the city is a bonus. Conveniently located right near the bus station. *Mon–Thu 7.30am–9pm, Fri/Sat 8am–10pm,*

Colonial architecture in Victoria: Marie Antoinette restaurant

Sun 9am–9pm | Maison La Rosière, Palm Street | tel. 458 01 19 | Budget

INSIDER TIP MARIE ANTOINETTE

What's special about this restaurant is the fact that there is only one (changes daily) Creole lunch and evening menu. Menus are therefore unnecessary, but you can still select individual items from the menu. Reservations essential! *Closed Sun | Grand Trianon | Revolution Avenue | tel. 426 62 22 | Moderate*

PIRATES ARMS

See and be seen: relax on the terrace – which faces on to the road – and indulge in some people watching as you observe the hustle and bustle around the Clock Tower in Victoria's centre. Culinary it is nothing special but there are reasonably priced snacks and refreshing drinks. Next door is a shopping arcade with a few small shops selling attractive souvenirs and there is also antique dealer. *Daily | Independence Avenue | tel. 422 50 01 | Budget*

SAM'S PIZZERIA

If you are longing for some Italian cuisine, this is your best bet. Even Italian guests consider these pizzas, which are baked in a stone oven, the best pizzas south of Sicily. But since there are also those who want to try something different, they also serve home cooked Creole dishes. *Daily | Francis Rachel Street | tel. 432 24 99 | Budget*

SPORTS & ACTIVITIES

The wide bay of Victoria lends itself to sailing and you can hire a boat from the *Marine Charter Association*. It is also possible to charter yachts without a local crew. The only golf course on Mahé the *Reef Golf Club* in Anse aux Pins *(south of the airport, 9 holes)*, is open to non-members and visitors need only pay the green fee. In Mont Fleuri there is a squash court at the Polytechnic as well as one in North East Point.

The lush tropical vegetation that surrounds all the hiking trails

HIKING ON MAHÉ ★

On Mahé there are a number of hiking trails with varying degrees of difficulty. The nature walks and trails are generally well maintained and are usually signposted so well that you cannot get lost. This is why you should follow the signs and not deviate from the path if you are not sure of the way. Another tip: don't walk too fast, rather take the time to admire the beauty of nature along the track. It is also advisable to let your hotel reception know the hike that you intend to take.

Some of the recommended trails on Mahé include the following: hike in the *Morne Seychellois National Park* along the rocky north-west coast of Mahé up to the small bay of Anse Major *(duration: there and back approx. 3 hrs | degree of difficulty: easy)*. The *Yacoa Nature Trail* starts at the end of La Misère Road, leads up and around the Dauban River, where you will have to cross several bridges (which have recently been repaired), you'll also see the tall Seychelles screw pine trees *(duration: there and back approx. 1 hr | degree of difficulty: easy)*. A demanding hike, which should only be undertaken if you are relatively fit, is the five hour hike up *Morne Blanc;* you will also need proper hiking shoes and weatherproof clothing. It is mostly a steep uphill climb but the rewards are worth it: magnificent views over the west coast of Mahé. On the way you can make a stopover at the INSIDER TIP *Tea Factory (Mon–Fri 7am–4pm | tel. 437 82 21)*, the only tea factory in the Seychelles (established in 1962), where you can take a guided tour (tickets 25 rupees) for information about the tea production, and then have a cup of tea afterwards. You can also buy the tea, of course ...

In Victoria's Botanical Gardens there are a series of brochures in the *National Parks &*

Forestry Section, detailing a total of 13 different hikes. The booklets don't cost much, but are sometimes out of stock.

ENTERTAINMENT

As a rule, the Seychellois go to bed early and it was only with the increase in tourism that the nightlife slowly developed, and the local youth are now also joining in. The popular discos are *Tequila Boom (Beau Belle | Victoria | Wed, Fri, Sat 10pm–6am)* and the open air disco, *Katiolo,* at Anse Faure *(Wed, Fri, Sat from 9pm)*. In the larger hotels on the island there is usually an organised entertainment programme; *Oceangate House* is popular for its *Amusement Centre* with its various slot machines and gaming tables. On Mahé there are two casinos: in the *Plantation Club* and the *Berjaya Beau Vallon Bay Beach Resort*.

WHERE TO STAY

There are no large hotels in Victoria, but instead there are charming guesthouses, often family run and with good local cuisine. Large hotels and resorts can be found under 'North Point/Beau Vallon' and 'Southern Mahé'.

HOTEL BEL AIR

A simple but comfortable guesthouse, in an old colonial mansion, with just seven air-conditioned rooms. Beautiful views over Victoria. *Bel Air | tel. 422 44 16 | www.seychelles.net/belair | Budget*

BEAU SÉJOUR

This small – there are only nine rooms – colonial style guesthouse is set in a gorgeous tropical garden. Nestled at the foot of a mountain, is has fabulous views of Victoria harbour and the outlying islands of the marine parks. And the rooms are tastefully decorated yet still quite reasonably priced. On request the owners will organise excursions to Mahé and the neighbouring islands. Only bed and breakfast, no restaurant. *Curio Road Bel Air | tel. 422 61 44 | beausejour_sey@yahoo.com | Budget*

INFORMATION

There is a Seychelles Tourism Board office on Mahé:

SEYCHELLES TOURIST OFFICE

Bel Ombre | P. O. Box 1262 | Victoria, Mahé | tel. 467 13 00 | www.seychelles.travel

TOURIST INFORMATION OFFICE CITY CENTRE

Independence House | Independence Avenue | Mon–Fri 8am–5pm, Sat 9am–midday | tel. 610 800

ISLANDS IN THE VICINITY

Seven islands lie off the coast of Victoria Bay; together they form the *Ste Anne Marine National Park*. The designation of the islands as a nature reserve was a matter of real urgency because the propellers of the ships entering and leaving Victoria unfortunately caused damage to the once magnificent underwater world. It is now a popular nature destination.

ANONYME

(121 E–F2) *(🕮 H12)*

In contrast to the other islands listed below, the large private island (40 acres) of Anonyme is no longer a part of the Ste Anne Marine National Park. It is located right in front of the airport on Mahé's east coast. Its location sounds worse than it is, because the air traffic is comparatively low. Large passenger planes only take off and land a few times a day. The *Anonyme Resort* changed hands in 2010 and the luxury resort that was previously on the island, as well as the restaurant, has since closed down. You can however, take a boat from Mahé and go to the island at high tide, which is what most of the local families do on weekends so that they can spend the day there swimming. When the tide is low you can wade the short distance to the island. While the island is privately owned the law stipulates that all beaches must be accessible to the public and the crystal clear waters off the island are ideal for snorkelling.

CERF ISLAND ★

(117 E–F6) *(🕮 F–G 10–11)*

Only 5km/3mi from Victoria, the island of Cerf is worth a visit just for its gorgeous beaches but it is also home to ● Caspar and Caroline, two old giant tortoises, who will patiently allow you to pet them. With approx. 300 acres the island is about the same size as Bird and Denis and was named after the French expedition ship 'Le Cerf', which had the famous Possession Stone on board.

The local tour operators offer excursion programmes which include barbecues on the beach, a meal at a restaurant or the opportunity to snorkel in the waters of the National Park. If you don't participate in an organised trip, you should reserve a table at *Kapok Tree (tel. 432 29 59 | Moderate)* or at *Restaurant aux Frères de la Côté (tel. 432 47 49 | Moderate)* and inquire about the ferries that pick guests up from the harbour in Mahé.

You can overnight at *L'Habitation des Cerfs* on the north coast *(14 rooms | tel. 432 31 11 | www.seyvillas.com/hotel-habitation | Budget)* or in the more exclusive, but also more expensive *Cerf Island Resort* on the south coast *(12 rooms | tel. 429 45 00 | www.cerf-resort.com | Moderate)*.

LONG ISLAND

(117 F5–6) *(🕮 G10)*

In the past access was only granted to those who had committed a crime: Long Island was once the prison island of the Seychelles. The Hong Kong hotel group Shangri-La Resort and Spa will soon be opening a luxury resort on the island. However, the opening date has yet to be confirmed. The reason for the latter is that the island's particularly restrictive environmental protection measures must be adhered to.

MOYENNE ISLAND

(117 F5) *(🕮 G10)*

Moyenne was also private property; in this case the island belonged to the former Australian newspaper publisher Brendan Grimshaw, who was able to generate some additional revenue with his small, well run *Jolly Roger* restaurant. Grimshaw passed away in the late summer of 2012, and the island is now known as the Moyenne Island National Park. Grimshaw built the hiking trail which covers a large part of the island, planted trees and also cared for the more than 100 giant tortoises on the island. He was also a tease with a good sense of humour, especially when tourists asked curious questions. There are two graves on Moyenne (which are believed to belong to pirates) and next to them is a pretty, wooden chapel. Inquire locally about the possibility of visiting the island.

ROUND ISLAND

(117 F5) (*📖 G10*)

Lazare Picault was the explorer that discovered this small island (only 50 acres and just 200m/660ft in diameter) and he named it Round Island due to its shape. It was once a female leper colony but now there are some superb diving and snorkelling sites around its coast. The island is currently only open for day trippers.

STE ANNE ISLAND

(117 E–F4) (*📖 G9*)

Ste Anne has a surface area of about 500 acres and is the namesake island of the Ste Anne Marine National Park. It has some historical interest because it was the first island in the archipelago that was settled by people. However, it is its other inhabitants that have aroused the interest of biologists: Ste Anne is a favourite nesting site for hawksbill turtles. From 1983 to 2001 the island was off limits but at the end of 2002 a five star hotel was opened by the Mauritian Beachcomber Group. The luxury *Sainte Anne Resort and Spa* has 87 private villas, some with private swimming pools. Facilities include a wellness centre with spa, sauna and massages as well as two tennis courts with flood-

Luxurious living under palm trees in Ste Anne Marine National Park

lights, all befitting a hotel of this standard. As the island is in a nature reserve, water sports are limited to non-motorised activities *(tel. 4292000 | www.beachcomber-hotels.com/sainte-anne-resort.php | Expensive)*. The resort includes a bar and five restaurants, such as the *Le Mont Fleuri* with Italian cuisine or the *L'Abondance.* Packages are all-inclusive.

NORTH POINT/BEAU VALLON

The road from Victoria leads via Beau Vallon Bay to the northern point of the island, North Point (116 A1) *(🕮 D7)*.

After a few miles heading south you reach Beau Vallon (116 A4–5) *(🕮 C–D 9–10)* and now you are in the area of Mahé with the most tourist facilities: here you will find a formidable selection of accommodation to choose from, such as the *Coral Strand Hotel* or the nearby *Le Méridien Fisherman's Cove*, with a beautiful stretch of pristine beach. The hotels also take full responsibility for the entertainment of their guests and organise evenings with folklore and music performances, often in conjunction with a Creole barbecue. This is not the place for discos, cinemas or nightclubs though.

It is worth driving a bit further from here, because shortly afterwards you will come across the place where the legendary pirate La Buse is said to have hidden a huge treasure shortly before his execution in 1730. Treasure hunters are still searching for it to this day. There is no public access to the gravesite but if you walk along the beach you will discover an INSIDER TIP

Here stress is a foreign word – the beach at Beau Vallon Bay

intricate system of canals and ditches. It is believed that La Buse hid his treasure in such a way that it would only be found at a specific water level.

FOOD & DRINK

INSIDER TIP BOATHOUSE

It is down to earth and multicultural here and you won't find a menu anywhere. The daily dishes are written up on a chalkboard. Open daily for lunch (midday–3pm) there is a set menu, a catch of the day and various curries, in the evenings a Creole buffet dinner is served from 7.30pm. You can keep going back until all the serving dishes are empty which is usually around 10pm. *Beau Vallon Bay | tel. 424 78 98 | www.boathouse.sc | Budget*

LA PERLE NOIRE

Sometimes the chef outdoes himself, at other times it is 'merely' an average Creole meal that comes out of the kitchen. Presumably it depends on the mood of the kitchen staff. There are also Italian and international dishes on the menu. *Mon–Sat 7pm–10pm | Beau Vallon | tel. 462 02 20 | Moderate*

LA SCALA ★ ●

One of the best restaurants on Mahé in a magnificent position on a rock at the southwestern end of Beau Vallon Bay. The Italian chef serves classic dishes including home-made pasta and fresh seafood. Expensive, but also very good! *Mon–Sat 7.15pm–9.30pm | Bel Ombre | tel. 424 75 35 | www.lascala.sc | Moderate–Expensive*

WHERE TO STAY

BEAU VALLON BUNGALOWS

The small complex has only twelve – but very pretty – rooms. Their restaurant is famous for its delicious Creole dishes and the owner also organises deep sea fishing trips and excursions to Silhouette Island. *Beau Vallon | tel. 424 73 82 | www.beauvallonbungalows.com | Budget*

BERJAYA BEAU VALLON BAY RESORT & CASINO

An upmarket complex that is also good value for money, with a beautiful beach and various water sports on offer. Creole and international cuisine is available in the restaurants. Casino, spa, sports and tennis courts. *232 rooms | Beau Vallon | tel. 428 72 87 | www.berjayahotel.com/mahe | Moderate–Expensive*

COCO D'OR

This friendly guesthouse is set in the midst of a grove of palm trees and practically right on the beach, with 27 air-conditioned rooms and friendly staff. *Beau Vallon | tel. 424 73 31 | www.cocodor.sc | Moderate*

CORAL STRAND

Completely renovated and reopened in 2011/12 this hotel is right on a lovely, long stretch of beach. It has beautiful rooms, is in a quiet location and has a nice piano bar. On the roof is the only public observatory in the Seychelles, which was previously operated in collaboration with the Laupheim National Observatory *(information at hotel reception). 140 rooms | Beau Vallon | tel. 462 10 00 | www.coralstrand.com | Moderate*

INSIDER TIP HANNEMAN HOLIDAY RESIDENCE

Just a short walk from Beau Vallon Bay lies this very well maintained, new guesthouse with seven large, fully-equipped apartments set in a beautifully landscaped and lush garden with swimming pool. The owners are happy to organise everything you need for your holiday in the Seychelles, including your rental car. There are shopping facilities for self catering as well as some restaurants nearby. There are also a number of local sporting activities in the area such as diving. *7 rooms | Nouvelle Vallée, Beau Vallon Bay | tel. 442 50 00 | www.hannemanholidayresidence.com |* Moderate

HILTON SEYCHELLES NORTHOLME RESORT & SPA

With brilliant views of the sea and one of the most beautiful beaches on Mahé, this Seychelles branch of the prestigious hotel chain is naturally rather pricey. If paying about 5000 rupees per night for one of the completely private luxury villas is not too much for you, then you may be inspired just like Ian Fleming was: he got his idea for the James Bond movie 'For Your Eyes Only' here. The vodka martini cocktail 'shaken, not stirred!' is of course also available at the bar ... *39 rooms | tel. 429 90 00 | www.seychelles.hilton.com |* Expensive

INSIDER TIP LE MÉRIDIEN FISHERMAN'S COVE

This thatch and stone five star hotel with all creature comforts was completely renovated in 2004; the rooms (all with sea views) are located either in the two storey main building or as chalets, set in lush gardens. *68 rooms | Bel Ombre | tel. 467 70 00 | www.lemeridien.com/fishcove |* Expensive

LE SANS SOUCI GUESTHOUSE

If you don't place a lot of value on being close to the beach and feel more at home in subtropical nature, you will enjoy this small guesthouse with only four pretty, spacious cottages. Nevertheless, the Beau Vallon Bay is still nearby, and it is only a ten minute drive by car or taxi to Victoria. There is a swimming pool and a restaurant that is well known for their Creole cuisine with magnificent views over Victoria and the neighbouring islands. *On the road from Victoria to Sans Souci | tel. 422 53 55 | sansouci@seychelles.net |* Moderate

SEYCHELLES YARRABEE

Small, family run, self catering guesthouse in Glacis with a spectacular hillside location. The house with three double rooms is particularly well suited for families with children, there are also several apartments. Beaches for bathing as well as shopping facilities can be found not far away at Beau Vallon Bay; the owners also provide car rentals and

THE GAUGUIN OF THE SEYCHELLES

Even if you cannot afford an original a visit to Michael Adams – the 'Gauguin of the Seychelles' – is almost obligatory. If the expat Englishman is not busy travelling the world opening one of his many exhibitions, you may get to meet the down to earth artist himself. His house on Mahé – with a small exhibition room where you can buy inexpensive prints – is just before Anse à la Mouche at Anse aux Poules Bleues *(Mon–Fri 10am–4pm | tel. 436 10 06)*. Works by Michael Adams now hang in many prestigious art galleries around the world.

lots of insightful travel advice. *Glacis | tel. 426 12 48 | www.seychelles-yarrabee.com | Budget–Moderate*

SPORTS & ACTIVITIES

At *Beau Vallon Bay* you can also find the greatest variety of sports on offer in the Seychelles: waterskiing, windsurfing, parasailing, fishing and dive trips and sailing boat rentals are all offered by numerous private companies as well as the large hotels.

SOUTH MAHÉ

With regard to the economy and tourism Mahé is geographically extremely 'top heavy' – the southern part of the island is still a true oasis of tranquillity in comparison to the north.

If you don't manage to visit another island during your holiday, you should at least explore the superb beaches and lush interior of south Mahé once.

SIGHTSEEING

ANSE INTENDANCE ★

(122 C5) (*🗺 G17*)

Right down in the south of Mahé lies Anse Intendance, possibly one of the most beautiful bays in the world. The long, wide beach is surrounded by impressive granite rocks and the sparkling water is crystal clear, making it ideal for swimming (from October to May). During the other months, there can be some large swell with waves breaking on the shore and swimming can be a rather perilous undertaking. You should definitely take heed of any warning signs and tips from the locals in this regard! A visit to Anse Intendance is better suited during the week because at weekends the beach is very popular with families. Above Anse Intendance is the luxurious five star *Banyan Tree Resort*, with 47 sumptuous private villas and all the conceivable creature comforts.

INSIDER TIP JARDIN DU ROI

(123 D2) (*🗺 G16*)

Of the numerous attractions on offer in the Seychelles, the Jardin du Roi (king's garden) is a small gem. Four well signposted trails lead through the landscaped private spice plantation. A hike gives you first-hand impressions of the spice trade of the archipelago. The small crêperie, which is part of the garden, serves delicious pancakes. *Near Anse Royale | daily 10am–5.30pm | entrance fee adult/child 110/55 rupees*

Exotic blooms in the Jardin du Roi

LA MARINE

(121 E–F6) *(H14)*

Model building enthusiasts will especially enjoy the faithfully recreated model frigates, schooners and warships made here. There are certainly cheaper souvenirs on offer in the Seychelles, but definitely not ones so lovingly made. An 18th century era model schooner will set you back about 17,000 rupees. At the arts and craft village, *Vilaz Artizanal (see below)* there is a branch with a workshop. *La Plaine St André | tel. 4375152 | Mon–Fri 7.30am–5pm, Sat 8am–5pm, Sun 9am–5pm*

Lovers of art and crafts are offered a great selection at the Vilaz Artizanal

POLICE BAY

(123 E6) *(H18)*

From Anse Intendance it is only a mile or so to Police Bay, yet another spectacular bay. Here the air is heavy with sea spray from the massive waves that crash on to the beach. The currents make swimming impossible and the danger signs should be taken seriously: some swimmers have paid with their lives for their daring. *On the southern tip of Mahé*

INSIDER TIP **VILAZ ARTIZANAL**

(121 E5) *(H14)*

The arts and crafts village, *Vilaz Artizanal,* was created by an initiative of Seychellois artists who decided to market their products collectively. They found a suitable plot of land at Anse aux Pins, against the scenic backdrop of a restored colonial house and in close proximity to the *Vye Marmit* restaurant they built small, neat wooden houses for their products. Besides decorative items (such as batik and pottery) there are also the usual souvenirs on offer. *Domaine de Val des Prés | Au Cap | tel. 4376100 | Mon–Sat 9.30am–5pm*

FOOD & DRINK/ WHERE TO STAY

BANYAN TREE RESORT

(122 C5) (🗺 G17)

This luxury resort, opened in 2001, was the first step in one of the government's programme to upgrade establishments on the island of Mahé, whose hotel standards had slipped in comparison to the other islands in the archipelago. Built by a Southeast Asian hotel group, the *Banyan Tree Seychelles*, with its 47 villas – each with private swimming pool – has little to fear from its competitors. To protect the environment the original, rather extensive plans of the investor were scaled back, but despite this the previously undeveloped Anse Intendance – one of the most beautiful bays in Mahé – has somehow lost its innocence through the building of the hotel. Having said this, a lot of care and attention is being given to environmental protection and sustainable tourism: electricity is largely generated with solar panels and they also have their own waste disposal. The hotel itself – for those who can afford it – will certainly fulfil nearly all your wishes which is why the guests are also understanding when it comes to the fact that they need to travel an hour by car or taxi to get to Victoria. *Anse Intendance | www.banyantree.com |* Expensive

CASUARINA BEACH HOTEL

(121 E5) (🗺 H13–14)

This small hotel with its 20 rooms is right on the broad, curving Anse aux Pins beach that is lined with tall palm trees. Very good value for money. *Anse aux*

BOOKS & FILMS

▶ **Seychelles – The Best of** – A beautiful coffee table book by international photographer Gregor Kervina that is a photographic journey of the pristine Inner Islands and their exquisite and unique nature. The book is available online from *www.seychellesbest.com*

▶ **Seychelles – Encyclopaedia of the Underwater World** – This book by Vincenzo Paolillo may be a little dated but there is no better compendium that details the impressive underwater world of the islands.

▶ **Wildlife of Seychelles** – A book by John Bowler that is an excellent photographic guide to all the fauna and flora of the Seychelles, lots of colourful wildlife pictures.

▶ **The Seychelles Affair** – This non-fiction book by mercenary Mike Hoare is an account of his abortive coup attempt (funded by the South African intelligence service) and his prosecution and subsequent imprisonment in a South African jail.

▶ **TV/Cinema** – the Seychelles is repeatedly used as a scenic backdrop for glamorous TV series, commercials and stills shoots: commercial directors swear by the picturesque boulders of La Digue and the secluded coves of Praslin.

▶ **For Your Eyes Only** – A collection of short stories by Ian Fleming featuring British Secret Service spy James Bond. One of the stories is set in the Seychelles.

Pins | tel. 437 62 11 | casuarina@seychelles.net | Budget–Moderate

FOUR SEASONS RESORT SEYCHELLES (122 A3) (*E16*)

A beautiful, world-class hotel and if you value refined luxury, you will feel right at home here. The resort's 67 private villas, each with their own small swimming pool, are situated on a slope so they all have unrivalled views over Petite Anse and the islands. There are two restaurants, serving Creole and international cuisine, a bar and a ● spa, where the therapies on offer include those made with local herbs and spices. *67 rooms | Petite Anse, Baie Lazare | tel. 439 30 00 | www.fourseasons.com/seychelles* | Expensive

KAZ KREOL (123 E2) (*H15*)

The small (but excellent) menu offers Creole and international cuisine, their speciality is their famed squid curry. The restaurant is run by an expat couple who are full of helpful hints for your Seychelles stay. You should reserve well in advance for dinner, as the few places are quickly filled. *Anse Royale | tel. 437 16 80* | Budget–Moderate

MAIA LUXURY RESORT & SPA (120 C6) (*F14*)

If you place a lot of value on a couple of thousand square feet of living space, want a butler around the clock and can afford to spare the necessary cash – then this exclusive resort is for you. The 30 private villas offer every comfort imaginable, each with private pool and view of the sea, all set in a unique landscape designed by American architect Bill Bensley. Guests are served meals by a Michelin-starred chef from Taiwan while the young generation enjoy the Jacuzzi or are pampered with chocolate massages. It goes without saying that there is also a magnificent private

beach and an extensive selection of water sports and activities – including ● yoga. *Anse Louis | tel. 439 00 00 | www.maia.com.sc* | Expensive

LE MÉRIDIEN BARBARONS (120 A4) (*E13*)

Relatively expensive, but set in gorgeous surroundings with 124 beautiful, comfortable rooms, almost all of which offer views of the sea. Two restaurants serve good international and Creole cuisine. *Barbarons | tel. 467 30 00 | reservations.barbarons@lemeridien.com* | Moderate–Expensive

LE RELAX HOTEL & RESTAURANT (123 E2) (*H15*)

Small hotel on a hillside with nine lavishly decorated rooms (air-conditioning, TV, mini bar, room service). Great views over the bay, highly recommended restaurant, and a swimming pool. The beach is just a

The secluded (and seldom crowded) Anse Royale in the south

short walk away and offers some excellent snorkelling. *Anse Royale | tel. 438 29 00 | www.lerelaxhotel.com* | Budget

INSIDER TIP VILLA BAMBOU

(122 C1) (*∭ F15*)

Only a very quiet little street separates this small guesthouse from Anse à la Mouche, one of the most beautiful beaches on Mahé. The three comfortable rooms are beautifully decorated and instead of energy-sapping air-conditioners, fans cool the air. The rustic guesthouse was built in an environmentally-friendly manner. Breakfast is served in the rooms on request and there are two restaurants in the vicinity. *Anse à la Mouche* | Moderate

VILLAS CHEZ BATISTA

(122 C4) (*∭ G17*)

Relaxed hotel with ten tastefully decorated rooms in four bungalows, their position on the stunning beachfront at Anse Takamaka is captivating. The restaurant offers Creole cuisine, especially fresh seafood. *Anse Takamaka | tel. 436 63 00 | www.chezbatista.com* | Budget

SPORTS & ACTIVITIES

In contrast to Beau Vallon Beach, the sports facilities in the southern part of Mahé are mostly limited to those at the hotels. However, most water sports are still possible. Some hotel owners also organise fishing trips; the catch then lands up – deliciously prepared – on the guests' dinner plates.

ENTERTAINMENT

The entertainment in the evenings is usually provided by the larger hotels: folklore shows, Sega music and sometimes a barbecue under the stars.

PRASLIN & NEIGH-BOURING ISLANDS

Radiating out from the main island of Mahé are a collection of 40 granite and two coral islands known as the Inner Islands. According to travel connoisseurs, the true Seychelles are to be found when you leave Victoria, and the main island of Mahé, and travel to these beautiful islands.

This is true in one sense but also not entirely true in another: while Mahé does have a well developed tourist infrastructure is still has some of what the other islands have to offer and if you choose Mahé as a holiday destination, you can always make INSIDER TIP day trips to the neighbouring islands.

ARIDE

(0) *(K–L1)* **All the things that money can buy: in 1973 the Scottish aristocrat and chocolate manufacturer Christopher Cadbury (1909–86) acquired the small (170 acre) granitic island of Aride, home to one million endemic sea birds.**

He bought the island as a reserve for the Royal Society for the Promotion of Nature Conservation and served as the society's president until his death. In 2004 the Island Conservation Society *(www.islandconservationsociety.com)* took over the island's management and opened a nature

Photo: Anse La Source à Jean, La Digue

Millions of birds can't be wrong: travel beyond Mahé and discover the pristine natural beauty of the Seychelles

conservation centre on Aride, where ornithologists research the world of birds. With conservation the island now has the ideal conditions for breeding and five bird species – once considered extinct – have returned *(www.arideisland.net)*. Now the birds can breed, lay their eggs and raise their young undisturbed. There are over a million sea birds (including the rare Noddy and Roseate Terns, Great Frigatebird and the White-tailed Tropicbird) that return here every year. Ten different bird species were counted by an ornithologist commissioned by the Seychelles government. ● Whilst he had access to the island at any time, tourists are only able to access Aride from Mondays to Fridays and only with an organised excursion, the weather must also be fair enough to make the landing in the small boats. The journey takes about two hours from Mahé (50km/31mi) and about 40 minutes from Praslin (10km/6mi). There is no regular boat traffic.

Cousin, a sanctuary for seabirds

Aride is the northernmost of the granite islands on the Seychelles Plateau and was discovered by Captain Nicolas Morphey in 1756. The name it carries today alludes to its climate: hot and dry. About a dozen inhabitants live in a small settlement on the island; they earn a living from the sale of guano.

Aride has a lush, tropical landscape with a great variety of plants. The guano enriched soil of the island is extremely fertile, evidenced by the fruits that grow here, such as lemons, oranges, bananas, and spices such as cinnamon, ginger and vanilla. There is a pathway for visitors (do not leave the designated route) that was designed to lead past all the interesting places with good viewpoints. Areas that are off limits (e.g. turtle nesting sites on the beach) are signposted. A nice nature trail also takes you up to the top of the 135m/443ft high hill where you will emerge from the woodland to have a magnificent panoramic view.

Another attraction (despite the coral bleaching events of 1998) is the ★ *underwater world off Aride.* A short time ago divers counted no fewer than 88 different species of fish during a single 90 minute dive. But even while just snorkelling you will get an excellent impression of the colourful underwater landscape.

There is no hotel or restaurant on Aride. Visitors bring a packed lunch along and enjoy a picnic instead. The picnic hut is also the only place where smoking is allowed on the island! You can only visit Aride with an organised tour group *(Mon–Fri | bookings via hotels or travel operators in Victoria)*. The fee including guided tour is about 500 rupees per person.

COUSIN

(O) *(🕮 K6)* **The tiny (only 70 acres) granite island of Cousin – not to be confused with the island of Cousine – is one of the last sanctuaries for bird species threatened with extinction.**

In 1968 the International Council for Bird Preservation bought the island and with the aid of World Wild Life Fund for Nature (WWF) made it into a nature reserve, one that is unique even for the Seychelles. The first goal was relatively easy to attain: to protect the few remaining specimens of the decimated Seychelles Warbler and Seychelles Weaver from extinction. This was a conservation success and populations of both birds can now be found on several of the nearby islands.

Today a lot is being done to return this almost circular island, that was once a dense deciduous forest, back to its original state. Man's sensitive intervention can be seen in the results yielded by nature: several dozen bird species now breed here. Cousin is also one of the best protected breeding grounds for hawksbill turtles in the world, has the highest density of lizards and even has a few giant tortoises. The best time for a trip to Cousin is during April or May, when hundreds of thousands of seabirds come here to breed.

There are a number of rules to be aware of on your visit to Cousin: do not stray from the designated pathways or remove anything from the island, all waste must be taken back with you, smoking is not permitted and it goes without saying that the birds and other wildlife should not be disturbed. Staying over on the island is also off limits!

The distance from Mahé is 44km/27mi so it is better to visit Cousin from Praslin or La Digue, where travel agencies and hotels organise the trips. Visitors are only allowed on the island from Mon–Fri between 9.30am–midday (closed weekends and public holidays), the boats go as close as they can to the island and then you have to transfer to a private island boat. The landing fee is about 500 rupees per person.

COUSINE

(O) *(🕮 J–K7)* **This is another island that attaches great importance to nature conservation. This small (60 acre) private island is one of the smallest granite islands and is home to a dozen specimens of the Seychelles White-rumped Shama and other very rare endemic birds.**

Hawksbill turtles also lay their eggs on Cousine, on the east coast the island has a very long sandy beach and from September

MARCO POLO HIGHLIGHTS

★ **Underwater world off Aride**
A record-breaking 88 species of fish seen in one and a half hours → p. 54

★ **Anse Victorin**
Frégate: an island idyll straight out of a glossy travel brochure → p. 57

★ **Island round trip**
By bicycle to the most beautiful places on La Digue Island → p. 58

★ **Granite rocks**
Picture-perfect: the boulders at Pointe Source D'Argent on La Digue → p. 58

★ **Anse Lazio**
On Praslin, one of the world's most beautiful beaches → p. 62

★ **Vallée de Mai National Park**
Dense, virgin forest with coco de mer palm trees → p. 63

to January the waters around the island have some excellent snorkelling. You can overnight at the *Cousine Island Resort,* a complex that consists of only four French colonial villas that can accommodate a maximum ten guests. The minimum stay is three nights (about 22,700 rupees per night, helicopter transfer from Mahé approx. 15 min) and included in the room rate is a sapling which you can plant in a selected spot. On request the local conservation officer will take guests around the island and explain the nature conservation initiatives. The resort has a swimming pool and a library and this is the ideal place for those looking for absolute peace and pure relaxation. *Tel 432 11 07 | www.cousineisland.com | Expensive*

FRÉGATE

(127 E–F 4–5) *(G–H 4–5)* **This charming little granite island was once the preferred hideout of pirates but today the exclusive Hotel Frégate Island Private with 16 villas (opened in 1998) is one of the most expensive hotels in the Seychelles.**

The island belongs to a wealthy German industrialist who not only values exclusivity but also protects and nurtures the environment, especially the last of the remaining Seychelles White-rumped Shama, making it popular with nature and bird lovers.

The island was named by Lazare Picault after the abundance of Great Frigatebirds (they have a wingspan of up to 2m/6ft) he found there on his second expedition in 1744. In the dense interior of the island there is an INSIDER TIP extraordinary diversity of plants and a large number of rare birds, the reason why Frégate has become a desired destination for ornithologists from all over the world. In 2012 the arrival of the Seychelles Warbler – a small songbird that only exists on four other islands on the Seychelles – marked the 100th bird species to make its home on

Frégate is ideal for some undisturbed sun, sea and peace and quiet

Frégate. Throughout the year there are about 40 ecologists and ornithologists working with the nature conservation on Frégate. They also offer guided ornithological hikes across the island. After a half hour walk you reach the *Mont Signale*, the highest point of the island, with a wonderful view.

And if you are looking for your dream beach, you will find it on Frégate. There are no fewer than seven of them here. South of the *Plantation House* lies *Anse Parc*, which is a wonderful place to snorkel at high tide, and in the opposite direction is ★ *Anse Victorin*, probably the most beautiful beach on Frégate. On the northern end of the airstrip is *Anse Bambou*, a beautiful small bay with white coral sand (warning: sometimes there are dangerous currents!). A nice walk leads to the opposite end of the island and to *Grand' Anse*, also a great snorkelling area at high tide. There is the great likelihood of coming across some of the island's 100 giant tortoises on the way.

FOOD & DRINK WHERE TO STAY

FRÉGATE ISLAND PRIVATE

With only 16 villas and prices of 57,000 rupees per night the hotel (which opened in 1998) is one of the most exclusive facilities on the Seychelles. Each villa has an area of more than 2000ft² and a private swimming pool, and there are two expensive restaurants and a spa. Bookings *www.fregate.com* | *Expensive*

SPORTS & ACTIVITIES

To snorkel you can either stroll to *Grand' Anse* or to *Anse Parc*, where there are still many INSIDER TIP intact coral reefs to explore. There is also a wide variety of water sports on offer.

LA DIGUE

(127 D–F 1–3) (*S–T 6–8*) **When you first leave the small harbour of Praslin, the powerful diesel engine drives the boat on but then the wind fills up the white sails. The crossing is a small taste of what awaits the visitor on La Digue – peace and calm.**

La Digue is often described as the most beautiful island in the Seychelles, and its many small, hidden coves and fine sandy beaches are well known around the world as the backdrop to countless advertisements. On the coast there are pristine beaches fringed by gigantic rock boulders, in the interior there are lush tropical plants – a package that captivates all its visitors. On La Digue there is no hustle and bustle – everything has its own very leisurely pace. Ox wagons are the mode of transportation but there are now also – perhaps regrettably – a greater number of taxis, which race through the narrow island streets.

Lazare Picault discovered La Digue in 1744 and named the island *Île Rouge* (red island) because of its reddish granite rocks. In 1768 the French captain and explorer, Marion Dufresne, gave the fourth largest island of the Seychelles the name of the command ship in his small expedition armada.

About 2200 people live on La Digue – and not only from tourism. The island has fertile soil, where coconut trees and aromatic plants (such as vanilla) thrive. There is no flight connection between Mahé and La Digue, the closest airport is located on Praslin. Flights take place several times a day. From Praslin there are two high-speed catamarans that run daily trips to La Digue and they only take about 30 minutes to cover the short distance.

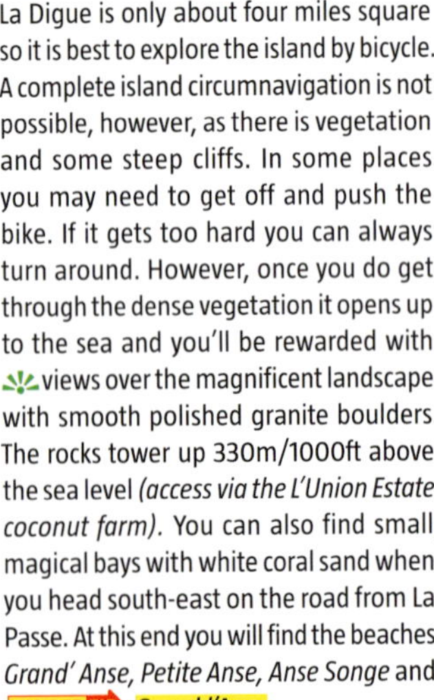

Powerful and bizarre: the granite rocks of Pointe Source d'Argent

SIGHTSEEING

ISLAND ROUND TRIP ★

La Digue is only about four miles square so it is best to explore the island by bicycle. A complete island circumnavigation is not possible, however, as there is vegetation and some steep cliffs. In some places you may need to get off and push the bike. If it gets too hard you can always turn around. However, once you do get through the dense vegetation it opens up to the sea and you'll be rewarded with views over the magnificent landscape with smooth polished granite boulders. The rocks tower up 330m/1000ft above the sea level *(access via the L'Union Estate coconut farm)*. You can also find small, magical bays with white coral sand when you head south-east on the road from La Passe. At this end you will find the beaches *Grand' Anse, Petite Anse, Anse Songe* and INSIDER TIP *Grand l'Anse*.

POINTE SOURCE D'ARGENT/ ANSE LA SOURCE À JEAN

(127 E3) *(S8)*

The mighty ★ *granite rocks* at the Pointe Source d'Argent could quite possibly be the most photographed boulders on earth and they feature in just about all of the advertisements for the Seychelles. Right behind them is *La Source à Jean*, a beach with pristine sand and crystal clear water. *Daily 7am–5pm | admission fee about 85 rupees*

L'UNION ESTATE

(127 E2) *(S8)*

From the ferry pier it is only a short walk south to the farm estate. It was bought in the 1970s by a German, Herbert Mittermayer. For many years he was considered a benefactor by the inhabitants of La Digue. He built a harbour jetty and an island hospital and had an irrigation system installed but in 1980 the estate was expropriated by President France Albert René. Today the farm currently provides jobs for 350 workers and during the week *(9am–4pm | 85 rupees)* there are demonstrations about the commercial use of coconuts such as the extraction of oil from coconut flesh. The farm also has four air-conditioned chalets (with half board) that are located right on a beautiful beach *(info/bookings: www.ladigue.sc | Moderate)*.

On the property there is also the recently renovated *Plantation House*, a fine example of French colonial architecture. It was built by the Hossen family, who came from Mauritius to the Seychelles and made their fortune by cultivating coconuts and spices. The house is open to the public *(Mon–Fri | 70 rupees)*, it is built with rare wood and has a roof thatched with palm leaves.

FOOD & DRINK

BERNIQUE (127 E2) (*S7*)

The restaurant belongs to the Bernique guesthouse. It is an attractive establishment serving local cuisine; on occasion they also have a Creole buffet. *Daily lunch and dinner | La Passe | tel. 4234229 | Budget*

LA DIGUE ISLAND LODGE

(127 E2) (*S7*)

The hotel restaurant serves (expensive) local and international cuisine. Occasionally a buffet is set up or a barbecue is organised. Nice bar with a great atmosphere. *Anse de la Réunion | tel. 4234232 | Expensive*

ZEROF

(127 E2) (*S7*)

Thanks to the delicious Creole cuisine it is also a favourite meeting place amongst the locals. *Daily 8am–10pm | Anse de la Réunion | tel. 4234439 | Budget*

WHERE TO STAY

BERNIQUE GUESTHOUSE

(127 E2) (*S7*)

Well maintained guesthouse set in the midst of a coconut grove, with five comfortable rooms. Anse la Passe beach is about a 15 minute walk away. The owner organises INSIDER TIP excursions in a glass-bottomed boat. *La Passe | tel. 4234518 | www.berniqueguesthouse.com | Budget*

CALOU GUESTHOUSE

(127 E2) (*S7*)

This is a relaxed guesthouse, with only five rooms. The restaurant serves Creole cuisine, there is also a bar, bicycle rental and boat trips. *La Passe | tel. 4234083 | www.calou-seychelles.com | Budget*

CHOPPY'S BEACH BUNGALOWS

(127 E2) (*S7*)

Small establishment near the jetty for the Praslin ferries. The ten bungalows are simple, but clean and are right on the beach. Half board is standard but full board is also available. *La Passe | tel. 4234224 | choppys@seychelles.net | Budget*

LA DIGUE ISLAND LODGE

(127 E2) (*S7*)

The largest (and most expensive) establishment on La Digue. This island retreat has a variety of accommodation options. There are 60 palm thatched chalets that are pleasant and comfortable as well as nine more rooms in *La Maison Jaune*, a colonial building built around the 1900s. Large swimming pool, scuba diving, snorkelling, boat trips, sunset cuises and ● bicycle rental. The in-house restaurant, *The Veuve*, offers excellent Creole and international cuisine. *Anse de la Réunion | tel. 4234232 | www.ladigue.sc | Expensive*

PATATRAN VILLAGE

(127 E1) (*🕮 S6*)
Attractive hotel with 18 comfortable bungalows located on a slope overlooking a small, picturesque bay. Traditional Diguois island dishes are served in the restaurant, once a week there is a lavish Creole buffet. *Anse Patates | tel. 4 29 43 00 | www.patatranvillage.com* | *Budget–Moderate*

ENTERTAINMENT

There is none of the usual organised evening entertainment on La Digue. After the sun sets (Anse de la Réunion is the ideal spot) you simply sit at the bar and sip an obligatory sundowner. As only a few streets are lit, you should remember to take your torch.

ISLANDS IN THE VICINITY

North-east of La Digue are four small islands, one of them, *Félicité* (O) (*🕮 U6*), was home to the Malayan Sultan of Perak who was exiled there in the 19th century for five years. Today this private island, which is only 3km/1.8mi from La Digue, has an exclusive hotel complex with two luxury bungalows and four equally comfortable chalets. Tennis, scuba diving, snorkelling and swimming are on offer, the restaurant serves exceptional Creole and international cuisine (*www.dreambeaches.com* | *Expensive*).
The other islands surrounding La Digue include Grande Sœur (O) (*🕮 U4*), Petite Sœur (O) (*🕮 T4*) and Marianne (O) (*🕮 W6–7*). They are ideal for swimming, snorkelling and hikes and are popular excursion destinations. You can reach Félicité and Marianne by boat from La Digue, the other islands from Praslin. Between Félicité and Grande Sœur lie three uninhabited islets: *Île Cocos, Île Platte* and *Île La Fouche.*

PRASLIN

(124–125) (*🕮 L–Q 4–7*) **The Vallée de Mai National Park on Praslin Island is an exceptional natural wonder, even by the rich natural beauty standards of the Seychelles, and if you miss out on a visit you will miss out on one of the greatest attractions of the Indian Ocean archipelago.**
With an area of just seven square miles, it is certainly not a giant amongst the world's national parks, but unlike any other it offers a dense concentration of the different plants typical to the Seychelles. This is what most of the islands of this archipelago must have looked like before the first Europeans settled on the Seychelles and set about intervening in the unspoilt nature that flourished here. No one knows why this valley was spared; it may well be the impenetrable vegetation or its seclusion deep in the island's interior. Whatever the reason – this large expanse of million-year old natural forest has remained almost entirely untouched. And there is hope that this strictly conserved area will preserve its state and appearance in the future. The Vallée de Mai with its unique coco de mer palm forest is one of the smallest areas to be declared a World Heritage Site by Unesco.
Praslin, with a length of 12km/7.5mi and a maximum width of 5km/3mi, is the second largest granite island in the Seychelles. Between Mahé, the main island (45km/28mi away) and Praslin there are numerous daily flights (time 15–20 min). There are also fast ferries that take about an hour to make the crossing.
After Mahé, Praslin is the most popular destination for visitors to the Seychelles. The island has a unique charm and a very peaceful atmosphere and offers a wide selection of accommodation in several resorts and hotels (both large and small)

that all blend in beautifully and harmoniously with the surrounding landscape. In the past the socialist government had restrictive policies that focused on the high-end of the accommodation market but these policies have been transformed in recent years. The state now not only approves of, but even promotes, private initiatives offering affordable rooms in guesthouses. Aside from the unique forest of the Vallée de Mai, Praslin also offers some truly beautiful beaches that frequently appear on the lists of the world's most exquisite beaches.

Until the arrival of tourism, the islanders lived from agriculture and fishing. Both still play a vital role, but nowadays the growing tourism industry provides employment for about half of Praslin's 7000 inhabitants. The island's main settlements are Baie Ste Anne and Grand' Anse. Baie Ste Anne is also Praslin's port and the arrival point of the inter island ferries.

SIGHTSEEING

ISLAND ROUND TRIP

By local standards Praslin has a rather good road network but tourists need to exercise caution as the driving conditions include left-hand drive, narrow roads and the lack of road shoulders. The roadside often drops a few feet straight down so drivers often veer off the road when swerving or trying to overtake! A good starting point for a round trip is the pier at the Baie Ste Anne, where the ferries leave for Mahé. If you take the road leading into the island interior, you will reach the area of the *Vallée de Mai* National Park after only a few miles. You drive a further 3km/1.8mi through a stunning, untouched landscape with towering mahogany and eucalyptus trees before you reach the entrance to the park. For those not wanting to drive, Praslin also has an efficient local bus service.

On La Digue tourists can be driven around on an ox cart

Huge palm trees in the Vallée de Mai National Park

ANSE LAZIO ★

(124 B2) (*🕮 M4*)

In the north of Praslin is Anse Lazio, a beach with powdery white sand, sparkling turquoise water and fringed with palm trees and dense lush vegetation. It is without a doubt the most beautiful beach on the island – and ideal for swimming and snorkeling – of course the word has spread and the beach is now very popular. Nonetheless you can still enjoy the views of the smooth, red granite rocks in crystal clear water. During the northwest monsoon the waves are several feet high.

ANSE POSSESSION

(124 C3) (*🕮 N5*)

From Baie Ste Anne the route continues along the coast via Anse Volbert to Anse Possession. It was here that Marion Dufresne erected the *Pierre de Possession* (Possession Stone) in 1768. With this act – also done by Captain Nicolas Morphey on Mahé in 1756 – Dufresne declared the island a French possession and gave the island its current name. The island was named after the minister of the navy at the time, Gabriel de Choiseul, the Duke of Praslin. The island, which you can see from Anse Possession, is called Curieuse. From here the road continues via Anse Boudin to Anse Lazio.

GRAND' ANSE

(124 C4) (*🕮 N6*)

The road that runs west from the Vallée de Mai takes you to the southern end of Grand' Anse, where the sea can be quite rough at times. It offers little in the way of scenic attractions, so it is better to continue along the coast towards the north, to Ste Marie's Point. From the crop of granite boulders, which you will reach after a short walk, you will have a wonderful view of the island and sea.

INSIDER TIP BLACK PEARL LTD.

(124 B3–4) (*M6*)

Opposite the Praslin Airport is a pearl breeding centre – the only pearl farm in the Indian Ocean – where the particularly beautiful black pearls are cultivated. You can visit the basins where mussels are kept and learn about the cultivation methods. In a small shop you can also purchase some pretty pearl jewellery. *Mon–Fri 9am–4pm, Sat 9am–midday | admission approx. 50 rupees | tel. 4233150*

VALLÉE DE MAI NATIONAL PARK ★ ●

(125 D4) (*O6*)

The best way to explore this idyllic World Heritage Site is by hiking the well maintained network of nature trails that run through the valley with its lush canopy of leaves. It is not permitted to leave the signposted pathways. Shortly after the entrance you can see a group of coco de mer palm trees that are estimated to be 800–1000 years old, almost certainly the oldest specimens of this botanical rarity. It is believed that there are about 6000 of these palm trees here. Naturally there aren't only coco de mer palms; botanists have counted 43 species – including all the palm species of the Seychelles and six endemic ones. With a little luck you may see the rare Black Parrot or one of the many small lizards that populate the Vallée de Mai.

A hike through the Vallée de Mai should take about 3–4 hours, but the paths are designed and signposted in such a way that you can always turn back and return to the starting point. More recently there is also a path that is suitable for wheelchair users. Along the main path is one that branches off and leads to a covered viewpoint overlooking the valley. *Daily 8am–5.30pm | admission approx. 300 rupees (cash only)*

FOOD & DRINK

BONBON PLUME

(124 B2) (*M4*)

Tourists and well off locals alike appreciate the excellent Creole cuisine served in this restaurant right on Anse Lazio. *Daily 12.30pm–3pm, dinner only on request and with a minimum of 10 | Anse Lazio | tel. 4232136* | Moderate

BRITANNIA

(124 C4) (*N6*)

This is a good option for a break during the island round trip; the excellent Creole cuisine is worth a stop. *Daily | Grand' Anse | tel. 4233215* | Moderate

INSIDER TIP CAPRICORN

(124 A3) (*L5*)

Even though the restaurant is a bit out of the way, the trip is well worth it for its widely praised, tasty and affordable local cuisine and delicious sorbets made from local fruits. *Mon–Sat 8am–11pm | Anse Kerlan | tel. 4233224* | Budget–Moderate

LOW BUDGET

▶ On Praslin it is a real pleasure to take a stroll on *Côte d'Or* at *Anse Volbert* in the evening when the temperature is perfect. On the way there are a few street restaurants with reasonably priced local specialities.

▶ Right opposite the jetty on La Digue is a supermarket where you can purchase Seychelles spice mixtures at affordable prices. The cooking instructions are sometimes quite funny ...

CHÂTEAU DE FEUILLES

(125 E5) *(🗺 P7)*

The exclusive hotel's restaurant serves excellent French and Creole cuisine; a speciality of the house is the grilled crayfish (a freshwater lobster) with garlic butter. Make your reservation well in advance! The unique views of the islands offshore of Praslin are an added bonus. *Daily, only evenings | Pointe Cabris | tel. 429 00 00 |* Expensive

SPORTS & ACTIVITIES

HIKING

Praslin is full of paths and just the right size for you to explore on foot. One particularly lovely hike leads from *Ste Marie's Point* to *Anse Lazio,* one of the most beautiful beaches in the Seychelles. However, you will need to take care as some of the paths are not maintained and are therefore difficult to follow. It is best to ask the locals for the right way. The hike begins at the bus station at *Ste Marie's Point,* buses leave there for *Grand' Anse.* Below the path, which leads through a lush landscape in a northerly direction, you will see the Anse Kerlan River, one of the rivers that traverse Praslin. On the bank to the north is a bridge over the river along a range of hills, and further on a steep pathway that leads down to *Anse Lazio.*

ENTERTAINMENT

There is a party atmosphere on Fri/Sat from 10pm at *Oxygen Nightclub* at Baie Ste Anne *(tel. 423 29 62)*, they have a dress code so make sure you are wearing something elegant. In some hotels and at the *Coco Bello* bands perform on Saturdays. Another hotspot is the *Jungle Club (tel. 451 26 83),* which is open on Fridays and Saturdays from 10pm: their motto is 'As wild as it gets'. Occasionally there are also live performances by the island's top local bands.

WHERE TO STAY

BEACH VILLA

(124 C4) *(🗺 N6)*

Small hotel with family atmosphere, the accommodation is in chalets right on the beach. Nine rooms with wonderful views of the neighbouring islands of Cousin and Cousine. Hotel staff organise boat trips to other islands, as well as deep sea fishing and snorkelling. *Grand' Anse | tel. 423 34 45 | martin@seychelles.net |* Budget

BERJAYA PRASLIN RESORT

(125 D3) *(🗺 O5)*

While this is not a five star hotel it is very popular due to its relaxed, friendly atmosphere. The 79 lovely rooms offer garden, sea and swimming pool views. Restaurant, three bars and a large swimming pool. Windsurfing, snorkelling and deep sea fishing are on offer. *Anse Volbert | tel. 428 62 86 | www.berjaya.com/praslin |* Budget–Moderate

HOTEL CAFÉ DES ARTS

(125 D3) *(🗺 O5)*

This mini hotel – it has just five rooms – is so pleasant and popular that you have to book early. Both the location, right on the beach, and the tastefully designed décor of the establishment are exceptional. It belongs to the artist Christine Harter and you can view her **INSIDER TIP** works and those by other artist in the small gallery. The spacious rooms are furnished in wood and have bathrooms with outdoor showers. There is also a small restaurant (lunch and dinner) that serves top quality seafood and decadent desserts. *Anse Volbert | tel. 423 21 70 | www.cafe.sc |* Budget

CHÂTEAU DES FEUILLES

(125 E5) *(🕮 P7)*

Not far from the ferry pier lies this beautiful, but relatively expensive hotel, with just nine luxurious suites. The hotel is surrounded by a large park, there is a swimming pool overlooking the sea and on weekends guests can take a boat trip to the private island of *Grande Sœur,* which belongs to the hotel. *Pointe Cabris | tel. 429 00 00 | www.chateaudefeuilles.com* | Expensive

CHAUVE SOURIS ISLAND LODGE

(125 D3) *(🕮 O5)*

At first glance one wouldn't suspect that there is a hotel on the tiny granite island off Côte d'Or. Surrounded by some massive trees and lush vegetation is a villa (with only five rooms) and a bungalow. The boutique hotel offers all the comforts with an all-inclusive package. Minimum stay is three days. All water sports available. *Chauve Souris Island | tel. 423 22 00 |* Expensive

The suites at the Hotel Coco de Mer have wonderful sea views

COCO DE MER

(125 D5) *(🕮 O7)*

The 52 spacious bungalows are set in a beautiful tropical garden bordering the sea. Particularly inviting are the comfortable, tastefully furnished INSIDER TIP *Black Parrot Suites* on a hill. There are fantastic views from their terraces! ● Wonderful massages with individually mixed oils. Point of departure for boat trips, a dive centre, jetty and squash court. *Anse Bois de Rose | tel. 429 05 55 | www.cocodemer.com* | Expensive

COLIBRI GUESTHOUSE

(125 E5) *(□ P7)*

A family run guesthouse with great view over the Ste Anne Bay, with 12 rooms. Diving excursions can be organised on request. *Pointe Cabris | tel. 429 42 00 | colibri@seychelles.net* | Budget–Moderate

CONSTANCE LÉMURIA RESORT

(124 A2) *(□ L5)*

Five star luxury hotel in a picturesque location on one of the most beautiful beaches in Praslin. Tasteful décor and particularly attractive suites. Restaurant serving Creole and international cuisine, spa and fitness centre, ● 18 hole golf course (the only one on the Seychelles). *115 rooms | Anse Kerlan | tel. 428 12 81 | www.lemuriaresort.com* | Expensive

INDIAN OCEAN LODGE

(124 B–C4) *(□ N6)*

Well maintained, spacious hotel complex on Grand' Anse with a magnificent garden. There are 32 very comfortable rooms in eight separate units. On the beach there is a highly acclaimed restaurant serving Creole and international cuisine. There are daily excursions to the neighbouring nature conservation islands of Cousin, Aride and Curieuse. *Grand' Anse | tel. 428 38 38 | www.indianoceanlodge.com* | Moderate

RAFFLES PRASLIN SEYCHELLES

(125 D5) *(□ O7)*

This luxury hostel was opened in 2011 and is part of the same hotel group as the legendary *Raffles* in Singapore. All of the modern villas have private swimming pools and views of Anse Takamaka and Curieuse Island. Restaurants, bars and perfect service all meet the legendarily high standards of the group. The spa has 13 treatment rooms offering all the therapies designed to uplift, soothe and restore your wellbeing. Numerous water sports and excursion trips on offer. *86 villas | Anse Takamaka | tel. 429 60 00 | www.raffles.com/praslin* | Expensive

LA RÉSERVE (125 D3) *(□ O5)*

Quiet hotel that is well suited to families due to its spacious and manicured gardens, but it is not cheap. The rooms are spread over several buildings, in front is Anse Petite Cour, a long private beach with many water sport activities. The Jetty restaurant is unique: it looks like a ship's pier, but has never been used as one. At least once a week there is an excellent Creole buffet that is open to both hotel guests and visitors. Book in advance and dress appropriately! *40 rooms | Anse Petite Cour | tel. 429 80 00 | www.lareserve.sc* | Expensive

VILLAS DE VOYAGEUR

(124 A3) *(□ L5)*

There are only two rooms in this lovely guesthouse at the end of Anse Kerlan, which you can see from the private terrace. Or you can sit in the beautifully landscaped garden and watch the sunset. They are fully equipped for self-catering and there are also shops nearby. On request the owner herself will create a special Creole meal. *2 rooms | Anse Kerlan | tel. 423 31 61 | www.villasduvoyageur.sc* | Budget

ISLANDS IN THE VICINITY

CURIEUSE

(124–125 C–D 1–2) *(□ N–O4)*

Just over a mile from Praslin is the tiny (one square mile) island of Curieuse, which received its name in 1768 from one of the ships on the expedition led by Marion Dufresne. The island is part of the Marine National Park and cannot be developed. It was once a leper colony, today only the warden and his family live here with about 250 giant tortoises. There are also numerous nesting places for the protected hawksbill turtles. Divers and snorkellers can find fantastic places in the coral garden at Pointe Rouge. Daily trips to Curieuse are offered by almost all the hotels on Praslin. The house on Curieuse was built in 1870 and served as home to the leper colony doctor, the building is now an *Eco Museum* and a *Visitor Centre (daily 8am–5pm | admission approx. 170 rupees)*.

So much better than by plane: taking a ship to Praslin

ROUND ISLAND (125 F4) *(Q6–7)*
Round Island (not to be confused with the eponymous island off Mahé) in front of the wide bay on Praslin's east side offers INSIDER TIP fantastic diving and snorkelling opportunities. Baie Ste Anne is only about 5km/3mi away and there are daily trips to the island from there.

DAY TRIPS
Operators on Praslin offer half day or full day trips to several neighbouring islands. On Cousin in the south-west and on Curieuse in the north, the pristine nature is the main attraction, and off St Pierre you can cool down at the end of the day by going snorkelling. Visitors are taken to the islands by boat and are then accompanied by guides on hikes across the islands. And the guides will gladly answer any questions you have. The hikes are not strenuous and the inclines gentle but you should still take plenty of water, sun block and insect repellent. Meals on the beach are included. The experience is unique, but not cheap *(approx. 1800 rupees)*. The landing fees that are on each island are one of the reasons for the steep price. But as these revenues benefit conservation, you should rather consider the fee a donation. There are a number of companies that offer the service so it is best to make enquiries at your hotel reception. Participants are collected by bus from the hotel.

BIRD ISLAND & DENIS ISLAND

You need both a deep wallet and a bit of luck to visit the two sister islands of Bird and Denis. The word is out that these two coral islands (just 50km/31mi apart from each other) are two of the great natural treasures of the Seychelles.

And as the accommodation is limited the islands are often quickly booked up and many tourists don't get to see them, which is a real pity. Yet again it may not be such a bad thing because this means that there is a good chance that the islands remain what they are meant to be in the first place: a retreat. Not merely for work-weary holidaymakers but also for the flora and fauna.

Whilst the largest part of the Seychelles consists of granite, Bird and Denis Islands are coral islands. Their seabed foundation is also granite but over centuries – perhaps even thousands of years – colourful corals have grown over it in all their splendour. A lot of sunlight, warm, clean water with plenty of plankton (the corals' favourite nourishment) and constant sea currents are the ideal conditions for the growth of corals. Protecting them should be a given. Unfortunately, over-exploitation has taken place over the past decades, not only underwater, but on the islands themselves. One example was the wholesale exploitation of guano, which was

Photo: Denis Island

Visiting Esmeralda and friends – seabirds, colourful corals and island landscapes straight out of a travel brochure

once used all over the world as a fertiliser. world. Up to 1905 a massive 17,000 tons of it was exported to Mauritius to fertilize the sugar cane fields. Today there is so little demand for guano, due to the availability of chemical fertilisers, that its removal can no longer be justified. Something that has had a positive effect on the nature as the flora and fauna have once again found an ecological balance.

BIRD ISLAND (ÎLE AUX VACHES)

(0) (M–N1) **'Is ★ Esmeralda still alive?' This is a question that the owner of Bird Island (also Île aux Vaches), approx.**

100km/62mi north of Mahé, has to answer quite frequently. And not without reason.

After all, this tortoise, with the rather curious – for a male – name of Esmeralda is believed to be over 170 years old (some sources even say 200 years old). He is

A rare White Tern on Bird Island

approx. 300kg/660lbs and 1.80m/6ft long and is the oldest known giant tortoise in the world. Esmeralda is undoubtedly the most prominent resident of Bird Island. The small island (1.5km/1mi long and 600m wide) was first known as Île aux Vaches (island of the dugongs) after the numerous sea cows that once lived in these waters.

Besides the tortoises, who are permanent residents of the island, two other species of marine turtles use Bird Island to lay their eggs: the hawksbill turtle and the green turtle. Because the Seychelles are the only place where these turtles can also lay their eggs during the day, there is no better place to observe them than here. Of course you need to be very careful, and follow all the rules so that you do not interfere with this unique natural spectacle.

This northernmost island of the Seychelles was discovered in 1756 by the Irish Captain Nicolas Morphey, who sailed to the Seychelles and annexed a whole series of islands for France at the behest of King Louis XV. Today Bird Island is privately owned and the owner certainly knows what he is doing. The 24 bungalows are often fully booked – a consequence of the company's philosophy that states you may only visit the island if you sleep over at least one night.

Bird Island is a coral island on the edge of the Mahé Plateau, not far from the edge of the island the plateau drops off to a depth of more than 1800m/6000ft. The island owes its tropical vegetation to the rich guano deposited by the tens of thousands of terns that regularly return here to breed. The resulting fertile soil is rich in organic compounds so not only do coconut trees flourish here but also mangos, papayas and avocados.

SIGHTSEEING

BIRD SANCTUARY ★

The northeastern part of the island is a bird sanctuary, and this is what makes the island such an attraction. You can view the birds from an observation deck – however, entering the protected area itself is not allowed. The most interesting time to visit is in the late afternoon or in the early evening when INSIDER TIP millions of Sooty Terns return from their daily forage for food at sea. Their excited chatter and clamour sounds for all the

world as though they are regaling their companions with the adventures of their day – that is the impression anyway! The Sooty Terns only require dry land from April to October, when they raise their young – they spend the rest of the year (at least according to the ornithologists) flying across the ocean. They sleep on the water at night.
Besides Esmeralda there is a second giant tortoise on Bird Island (and about 40 human inhabitants). Both tortoises do not come from here though, they were brought here a long time ago from the far distant Aldabra Atoll.

FOOD & DRINK WHERE TO STAY

BIRD ISLAND LODGE

The lodge's palm-thatched bungalows have spacious and attractively furnished rooms, with small terraces overlooking the sea. Delicious Creole meals are served in the restaurant. *24 bungalows | information and bookings (only full packages) in Victoria on Mahé: P. O. Box 1419 | tel. 4224925 | www.birdislandseychelles.com | Expensive*

SPORTS & ACTIVITIES

As long as you don't disturb the birds, you are given free rein to enjoy yourself at leisure. The hotel owner offers guests a motorboat for deep sea fishing excursions and there is excellent snorkelling in the clear waters off the southern part of the island at high tide.

ENTERTAINMENT

Don't expect exciting evening entertainment on this peaceful island. A good book, a decent bottle of wine and some stimulating conversation with other island guests is ample compensation for any lack of nightclubs and bars.

DENIS ISLAND

(0) *(🕮 O–P1)* **Denis Island is as flat as a pancake and a mere half a mile square and from here it is only about another 8km/5mi to the area of the seabed where the coastal Mahé Plateau drops down 1800m/6000ft.**

The island only rises about 3.50m/12ft out of the sea and is completely surrounded by a protective coral reef – a INSIDER TIP fantastic area for snorkellers and divers. In contrast to most of the other islands, which rise from the underwater granite plateau, Denis is a genuine coral island that came into existence a lot later than for example La Digue, Praslin or the main island of Mahé. Denis is privately owned,

MARCO POLO HIGHLIGHTS

★ **Esmeralda**
A celebrity giant tortoise that has legendary status for being at least 170 years old → p. 69

★ **Bird sanctuary**
Take a guided tour of the north-east of Bird Island – ornithology included → p. 70

★ **Denis Island round trip**
Through the dense forest to an old lighthouse → p. 73

★ **House reef off Denis**
Not far from the shore a reef with a 30m/90ft drop – exciting for divers → p. 73

No better place for sailors: a catamaran off Denis Island

and that is also the reason why you can only book a flight to the island when you have made a reservation to stay overnight. Exclusivity is the trump card here – and this is reflected in the steep room rates of about 16,000 rupees per night.

There is also an interesting myth that a pirate's treasure has lain hidden for centuries somewhere on Denis Island. Several treasure hunts here – and on other islands – have thus far all been unsuccessful. However, the skeleton of

SMILE PLEASE!

The inhabitants of the Seychelles are very open and are generally happy to have their pictures taken, nevertheless you should always first ask their permission. The diverse natural landscape also offers countless interesting images. Each island has its special charms: the fantastic beaches on Mahé, the granite boulders on La Digue – shaped over the centuries by the wind and weather – or the unique World Heritage Site of Vallée du Mai on Praslin. And if the camera's memory card is full, there are plenty of supplies in the shops in Victoria on Mahé (such as at *Home2Office | Premier Building*). Do bear in mind that taking photographs of people during religious rites or disturbing a religious service is highly inappropriate! Professionals take their shots usually in the early morning or late afternoon when the light is at its best. Sun, fine sea sand and seawater are the worst enemies of valuable camera equipment so you should always cover all your lenses after taking your photographs and keep your camera securely in its case.

a man (whose identity is still a mystery) was discovered.

You can either reach the island with the supply boat that travels regularly between Mahé and Denis, or if necessary, with the plane that operates daily. Full packages are available at the travel agencies in Victoria on Mahé. The flight only takes half an hour.

SIGHTSEEING

DENIS ISLAND ROUND TRIP ★

Denis Island is almost completely covered by a dense forest of Kasuarina and Takamaka trees and coconut palms. You shouldn't expect any special botanical rarities or anything sensational during a trip around the island, which should only take you about an hour and a half at a leisurely pace. But you can observe a few giant tortoises and, if you have a keen eye, you may also spot a few pretty, colourful tropical birds in the trees. At the northern tip of the island is a lighthouse dating to the turn of the century and two deserted stone buildings that once probably served as a prison.

FOOD & DRINK
WHERE TO STAY

DENIS ISLAND LODGE

The 25 bungalow resort offers all the creature comforts and is located on the west coast of the island, near the airstrip. The only restaurant is operated by the hotel. The cuisine served is delicious as almost all the ingredients are grown on the island itself and are therefore always wonderfully fresh. *Denis Island Lodge | reservations (Victoria) 429 59 99 | www.denisisland.com | Expensive*

SPORTS & ACTIVITIES

Denis Island is surrounded by fine but rather narrow sandy beaches. The island's real attraction is underwater off the western coast: not far from the shore is the ★ Denis house reef where, at depths of up to 30m/90ft, you can find an extraordinary variety of sea creatures. The area around the island is apparently teeming with fish. Interestingly the damages that were caused by the global climate phenomenon of El Niño in 1998 are only visible in exposed areas. Although renowned marine biologists predicted that it would take many years for the corals to recover from the sudden flow of warm water, many of the soft corals are growing back. In terms of sports activities, there are sailing boats, surfboards and fishing equipment on offer and there is also a spa.

ENTERTAINMENT

All the trials and tribulations of your everyday life will melt away when you enjoy a spectacular Seychelles sunset. Nightlife? Unfortunately not!

SILHOUETTE & NORTH ISLAND

No matter whether you only do a day trip or if you choose this lush and mountainous island (seven square miles) as your holiday home: a visit to Silhouette Island, off the north-west coast of Mahé, is a holiday must.

This is probably how Mahé looked before man arrived and intervened in nature: it is characterised by dense rain forest and lush, tropical flora that gives it a similar feel to Mahé, which has three mountains with a height of more than 500m/1640ft. At a height of 751m/2460ft INSIDER TIP Mount Dauban is the third highest mountain in the Seychelles. A strenuous hike to the summit of the mountain will be rewarded with some dramatic scenery and a wonderful view of Mahé.

The fauna is just as diverse as the flora and in addition to several dozen giant tortoises there are the countless bird species, which you can see when you do your leisurely trip around the island. Silhouette is only 18km/12mi away from Mahé, is made of pure granite and is the third largest island of the Inner Islands. There is no airport on the island as the landscape is too mountainous and it is very close to the main island of Mahé.

It is more complicated to get to the North Island. The unspoilt, tropical island is pri-

Photo: Hilton Seychelles Labriz Resort on Silhouette

The islands are popular with hikers: dense rain forest, tropical vegetation and pristine beaches in exclusive seclusion

vate property and can only be visited with permission or as holiday accommodation. Aimed at well heeled guests, it is one of the world's most expensive retreats (approx. 50,000 rupees per person/night) and ensures total luxury, privacy and exclusivity for its clientele. North Island is located 6km/3.7mi from Silhouette and 25km/15.5mi from Mahé (transfer by helicopter).

SILHOUETTE

(126 A–C 1–3) (*🕮 A–C 5–7*) **The island is named after the French Finance Minister, Etienne de Silhouette, who apparently decorated his house with (cheap) silhouettes instead of (expensive) paintings and in so doing also gave this silhouette its name.**

Europeans first discovered the island in 1767 but there were probably Arab seafarers on the island several centuries before. The island's history is inextricably

The pitcher plant is one of the carnivorous plants found in the Seychelles

linked with the history of the Dauban family, who immigrated to the Seychelles from France in the mid-19th century. Auguste Dauban became wealthy through the trade with copra and coconut plantations and bought the island of Silhouette. Around 1860 he constructed a wonderful house made of Takamaka wood which was called *Grande Case* by the island locals. It was furnished with exquisite furniture, and they ate from the finest Chinese porcelain. The Dauban family line has died out but one of the last in the dynasty line participated as javelin thrower at the Olympic Games in Paris in 1924 thanks to the skills he acquired as a child harpooning for fish in the reefs of Silhouette. Today there are three small villages with about 200 inhabitants, who live mainly from the coconut harvest. They produce copra from the coconut flesh. They also cultivate spice plants, coffee, tobacco and tropical fruits. Since the construction of the luxury hotel, the *Hilton Labriz*, new jobs have also been created in tourism. The island itself is – besides the parts around the harbour – not easily accessible and therefore serves as a home for many rare plants.

Even though the villages are all along the coast, it is often not possible to reach them by boat across the water due to rough swell. Therefore the only choice for residents and visitors is to take the rather arduous route through the forest. Silhouette can easily be reached via the channel (rich in fish) that separates the island from Mahé. Boat owners at Beau Vallon Beach offer day trips and also have fishing equipment on board (so lunch is assured). The passage takes about an hour.

SIGHTSEEING

ANSE MONDON ●

(126 A–B1) *(🕮 B5)*

Anse Mondon on the north side of Silhouette is *the* picture-perfect beach, one that is well known from postcards. However, you need to bank on about a two hour walk to get there and in places the path leads over smooth rocks, so it is best not to set out when it is raining. The reward for the hike is the sight of one of the most beautiful beaches in the Seychelles. Remember to take your mask and snorkel so you can also explore its fascinating underwater world.

ARAB GRAVES ★

(126 C3) (🕮 C6)

Thirty graves at the *Anse Lascars* are silent witnesses to the fact that Arab seafarers arrived on the island from about the 9th century. You can combine a visit to the graves with a very interesting hike through the lush, overgrown nature. Just follow the path that starts left of the harbour; it leads along the coast and ends abruptly at a high rocky reef. A short walk from the harbour is the INSIDER TIP Dauban family tomb and mausoleum. A marble plaque at the entrance bears the inscription, 'Dying is not dying, my friends, dying is just change ...' On the way you will undoubtedly come across a few giant tortoises and – if you pay careful attention – you may also see a few tropical birds in the forests below Mont Gratte Fesse.

SILHOUETTE ISLAND ROUND TRIP ★

You should plan on at least half a day for an island round trip. It is best to employ a guide (available at the harbour) so they can lead the way as the route is sometimes steep and the paths confusing. As compensation for the somewhat strenuous hike you will get to experience an impressive and largely unspoilt landscape with a rich variety of plants and animals. One such botanical rarity is a carnivorous INSIDER TIP pitcher plant that is endemic to the island; there are several beautiful specimens on Silhouette.

LA PASSE

(126 C2) (🕮 C5)

If you come by boat from Mahé, the small village of La Passe is the first port of call on the east coast of Silhouette. Opposite is an old house that is one of the most beautiful old style colonial houses in the Seychelles, the houses of La Passe are to the right.

FOOD & DRINK WHERE TO STAY

LA BELLE TORTUE

(126 C2) (🕮 C5)

The *La Belle Tortue* also places a lot of emphasis on exclusivity and privacy. In the lodge there are nine remarkably plush rooms, as well as a restaurant right on the beach, a bar, a spa and a dive school nearby that runs PADI courses. There are daily excursions for divers and snorkellers. *Tel. 432 53 35 | www.labelletortue.com | Moderate–Expensive*

HILTON SEYCHELLES LABRIZ RESORT & SPA ★ (126 C1–2) (🕮 C5)

The only hotel on Silhouette Island also happens to be one of the finest establishments that can be booked in the Seychelles. Along the mile long, sandy beach of Anse La Passe are 111 chalets, the smallest almost 1000ft², the largest

MARCO POLO HIGHLIGHTS

★ Arab graves
Inscriptions may be hard to decipher – but the Arabs really were there → p. 77

★ Silhouette Island round trip
Visit an indigenous carnivorous plant → p. 77

★ Hilton Seychelles Labriz Resort & Spa
The only hotel on Silhouette, but a superb one! → p. 77

★ North Island Resort
Kate and William spent their honeymoon here – when are you coming? → p. 79

nearly 2000ft², all with their own private garden and swimming pool. Everything you expect of a five star resort is on offer here. Pamper yourself with spa treatments in the wellness centre, exert yourself with one of the many water sports or join a guided nature walk. The on site dive centre regularly organises trips out to pristine underwater dive spots. There are no less than five top class restaurants that offer culinary delights from all around the world. *Reservations in Victoria: tel. 429 39 49 | www.seychelles labriz.hilton.com | Expensive*

NORTH ISLAND

(O) *(B–C1)* **A remarkable feature of this small (2km²/500 acres) densely verdant island are its three magnificent granite 'mountains'. They reach a height of 214m/700ft above sea level. North Island – Île du Nord in French – is ideal for walking and hiking.**

In 1609 North Island was the first granite island in the Seychelles to be explore by Europeans, but this first – British – expedition was not without consequence. Thereafter the coves and caves along the coast became the ideal hideouts for pirates on the lam. On a trip around the world the well heeled British amateur botanical artist, Marianne North, stopped off here and her impressive Seychelles paintings can still be admired in England to this day.

The first settlers on North Island made their living from the cultivation and processing of coconuts and other fruits. When the coconut industry lost its importance at the end of the 19th century, they left the island. The island became overgrown with weeds and infested with rats and vermin. Even the indigenous wildlife nearly died out. Then in the mid 1990s it was rediscovered by a private investment group from South Africa who decided to not only make the island a haven for well-heeled guests, but also to start a remarkable nature conservation project. The initiative has meant that the natural habitat has been fully restored and there are now many indigenous animals, especially birds, who have once again settled here. The management also wants to make

SEYCHELLES COMPACT

Each island in the Seychelles has its own charms, and you shouldn't limit your visit to only one of them. The best option is to do some island hopping in the Inner Islands and there are various organisations available to you. The ships are not the large ocean liners, but agile sailing boats such as the 'Sea Shell', the 'Sea Bird' or the 'Sea Star'. They take a maximum of 16 passengers and also stop along the way to give you the opportunity to have a swim or go for a dive. Accommodation and full board are included, and a number of islands are visited and separate trips to them would otherwise have cost a lot more money. The bottom line is that these cruises are a fairly inexpensive alternative to a hotel vacation. A popular option is to combine the both. *Information: www.seychelles-cruises.com*

North Island energy-neutral by means of solar power and the collection of rainwater – on a rainy day as much as 30,000 litres of water can be collected.
North Island is one of the most fertile islands in the whole archipelago. Only a few years ago almost 100 residents still lived from vegetable cultivation, livestock and fishing. Until the opening of the new North Island Resort there was no place for tourists to overnight.

Pleasure in paradise: cruising on board the 'Sea Shell' traditional schooner

WHERE TO STAY

NORTH ISLAND RESORT ★

Opened in 2003, this five star resort has eleven bungalows and belongs to the category of resorts – similar to the resorts on Frégate and Cousine – that offers its guests the ultimate in luxury in the midst of unspoilt nature. The bungalows are along the flat coast and are shielded from each other. The management places great importance on letting their visitors know about the continuous environmental measures taken to ensure nature conservation despite the fact that they are running a hotel business. The guests receive detailed information and can talk to any of the researchers and the nature conservationists working here. The high price of accommodation is justified with the argument that a large proportion of the income goes back into the environment and nature conservation. The hotel is marketed by a South African company. *www.north-island.com* | *Expensive*

OUTER SEYCHELLES

The journey is admittedly a little long and difficult but those who venture out will be richly rewarded, because the atolls and islands of the Outer Seychelles create an unusual contrast to what is usually defined as typical of the Seychelles.

These islands do not consist of granite but – just as Denis and Bird Island – they are the product of corals that have been growing for thousands of years. In contrast to the islands of the Inner Seychelles they are not on the underwater Mahé Plateau described in the introduction, but are a good 200km/125mi south-west of the main island Mahé.

The islands of the Outer Seychelles are among the finest that the archipelago off the African coast has to offer: beaches with sand like powder, crystal clear water and a fascinating underwater world. It also appears as though nature has recovered faster from the destruction created by the 1998 El Niño climate phenomenon than was predicted.

The Farquhar Group of the Outer Islands has their own flora and fauna world, one that seems rather modest in comparison to the islands rich in species that you find elsewhere on the Seychelles. However, their underwater world is interesting, presenting exceptional diversity, because

Photo: Cave diving off Desroches

Coral islands with spectacular beaches and a fascinating underwater world: paradise has a name

the Farquhar Group consists primarily of flat coral islands, scattered over a surface area of 40mi². Coconut palms grow on the islands – such as on Providence Atoll in the northern part of the Farquhar Group and on the main island of Providence – and are exploited commercially. Several contract workers also live here, but there is no accommodation for visitors. The journey there is also not easy, as the small island airport is only used for individual charter flights. If you are interested, the best contact is the *Island Development Company (IDC)* in Mahé *(tel. 422 46 40 | idc@seychelles.sc)*.

However, there is another option to get to the Outer Islands and the islands of the Farquhar Group. They are a popular destination for sailing trips, and the local skippers know exactly which islands are

Giant tortoise on the Aldabra Atoll

allowed to be visited and those that are off limits due to nature conservation restrictions. However, it is very important that you find out the current security situation from the tourism authorities on Mahé (or *www.seychelles.travel*) before undertaking such a trip. In 2010 this remote region was beset by Somalian pirates who seized a tourist boat for ransom and only released it once their financial demands were met.

ALDABRA ATOLL

(126–127 A–E 4–6) *(📖 A–E 17–18)* **The islands of the Aldabra Atoll are located – far outside of the Mahé Plateau – on a basalt foundation about 1000m/3300ft deep under the sea. The foundation rose upwards about 80,000 years ago, presumably through a volcanic eruption – and sank again leaving the edge of the crater.**

There are only 20 residents on the 14 islands that form the atoll: Grande Terre, Île Dubois, Îles aux Cèdres, Îlot Emile, Île Esprit, Îlot Lanier, Îlot Magnan, Île Moustiques, Îlot Parc, Île Michel, Malabar, Picard, Polymnie and Îlot Yangue.

The largest islands are Grande Terre (South Island) and Malabar (Middle Island); altogether the Aldabra group comprises a land surface area of just 60mi². The entire island of Mahé could fit into the lagoon. If you combined the total area of land and lagoon, the Aldabra Atoll would be the largest in the Indian Ocean with 140mi².

Hard to believe and yet true: if it were up to British strategists, today there would be a military base in the Aldabra Atoll. However, this did not come to pass thanks to the Labour cabinet in London that campaigned in 1971 to surrender any military presence east of the Suez Canal. And so the Aldabra Atoll was spared that fate.

The isolation of the atoll is probably the most significant reason for the preservation of its unique flora and fauna. Aldabra was already known to Arab seafarers in the 9th century as the name *alkhadra* (the green one) suggests. Later, around 1502, the explorer Vasco da Gama visited the Aldabra Atoll for a few days. In more recent history Aldabra was first sighted by Lazare Picault in 1742. Afterwards the island was visited every now and then by ships passing by, but the landing was difficult, the terrain inhospitable, and there was no fresh water. Potential settlers left to continue their journey after a short stay. Only a few Chinese settled here at the beginning of the 20th century to gather the fibres from the sea cucumbers which are considered a delicacy in the Far East. Parts of the mangrove forest were cut down and vast numbers of tortoises and turtles were killed – also for consumption.

The Aldabra Atoll is considered the home of the ★ *giant tortoises.* At the beginning of the 20th century they were close to extinction. Thousands of tortoises landed in soup pots of eccentric gourmets all over the world. The naturalist Charles Darwin was the first to point out the danger of extinction; he saw the animals as living witnesses of a bygone era of earth's history. They are said to have survived 200 million years without any significant change in their appearance.

Today the giant tortoises enjoy strict environmental protection and their population has fortunately recovered once again. On the entire atoll there are now almost 150,000 tortoises while there are also some turtle species that visit as temporary guests when they arrive here to lay their eggs from December to March. Tortoises are omnivores, but their main diet consists of plants and grasses.

The fact that the Aldabra Atoll has been a Unesco protected World Heritage Site since 1976 also means that access is not that easy and requires special permission. This is included if you participate in an organised expedition, such as the 'Indian Ocean Explorer' *(www.ioexpl.com)*. You can find out more current information at the tourist office at the Independence House in Victoria on Mahé. This also applies to the current situation regarding the dangers of raids by Somalian pirates on tourist ships and sailboats. As there are no tourist facilities, you either have to sleep over on the boat or continue your journey on the same day. The trip on the 'Indian Ocean Explorer' costs about US $325 a day per person, the charter flight to Assumption US $1000.

If you are given approval to access the islands in the atoll, you will encounter some remarkable nature: INSIDER TIP more than 270 different plants live here, of which about two dozen are endemic. Botanical specialities such as the Aldabra Lily and the Aldabra Screwpines are quite remarkable. But you have to have a keen

MARCO POLO HIGHLIGHTS

★ Giant tortoises
The Aldabra Atoll is believed to be the true home of these mighty reptiles → p. 83

★ Mushroom islands
The Aldabra Atoll is characterised by mushroom-shaped stone formations → p. 84

★ Underwater world
The hauntingly beautiful underwater world off Desroches → p. 86

★ Desroches Island Lodge
Rest, nature, luxury: leave your cares behind → p. 87

eye, because at first glance the flora doesn't appear to be very spectacular and seems limited to mangroves, coconut palms and shrubs. There is also a rich variety of fauna, including dozens of bird species, such as the White-throated Rail, the last flightless bird in the Indian Ocean, or the Aldabra Drongo, a songbird that is found only on the Aldabra Atoll. The diversity of the flora and fauna endemic to the Aldabra Atoll is down to its status as a Unesco World Heritage Site.
The lagoon, fed by four channels from the sea, has a tidal range of up to 3m/10ft and during low tide the lagoon is almost dry. Then you can see the strange and bizarrely formed ★ *mushroom islands*: limestone slabs that have been eroded by water at the base.

AMIRANTE ISLANDS

(0) (*🕮 0*) **This chain of coral islands forms part of the Outer Islands, which stretch from the interior of the Seychelles out towards the African mainland. The main island of Mahé is situated the closest to the chain; the distance from the Amirante isle closest to Mahé is only 220km/140mi.**

Several archipelagos fall under the Amirantes and include: Alphonse, D'Arros, Rémire, Boudeuse, Desnœufs, Desroches, Étoile and Marie Louise as well as the island groups of the African Banks, the St Joseph's and Poivre atolls. All the islands in the Amirantes are a paradise for seabirds. On Desnœufs for example there are massive colonies of Sooty Terns and it is INSIDER TIP particularly busy during the breeding season from May to July. Some of the bird's eggs are collected and taken to Mahé as they are considered a delicacy.

The Amirantes are mostly made up of small islands and islets, coral reefs and sandbanks, which collectively have a surface area about 4mi². They were first discovered by Arab seafarers about 1000 years ago, the discoveries were probably unplanned when their ships accidentally ran aground in the shallow waters. Later, in 1502, the Portuguese explorer Vasco da Gama gave the island group its current name during his second journey to India. It was also he who had more detailed nautical charts drawn up, with even the small sandbanks marked. The current names of the islands cannot be traced back to Arabic or Portuguese origins as the old names were replaced by French names during the colonial era. In 1814, when England and France signed a peace treaty, the Amirante group of islands became part of the English colony of Mauritius, which also included the Seychelles as a whole. Finally, in 1909, when

Deserted beach on the coral island of Alphonse

the colonial era ended, the Amirantes became part of the Seychelles.

ALPHONSE (O) *(🗺 O)*

The three islands in the Alphonse group extend over about 16km/10mi. The island group is named in honour of the explorer Chevalier Alphonse de Pontevez; St François, the name of the neighbouring island, was named after St Francis de Sales. The triangular coral Alphonse Island is about 1.2km wide and lies at the edge of the lagoon, which is very inviting for a swim and is full of fish and turtles. The island is covered by dense groves of coconut palms. Also interesting are the overgrown sisal and cotton wool plantations that date back to the 19th century. The barrier reef is ideal for snorkelling and Alphonse has also become a paradise for fly-fishing.

The recreational options on Alphonse itself are limited, but the island offers a good point of departure for excursions to the islands of the neighbouring atolls of *Bijoutier* and *St François* (approx. 1350–2000 rupees). Snorkelling trips cost about 450 rupees, sundowner cruises are about 850 rupees and fishing trips about 1200 rupees.

The *Alphonse Island Resort,* on the edge of the lagoon, is currently the accommodation that is the furthest from the main island on the Seychelles. It offers a total of 30 chalets in two categories (completely renovated in 2012) and has a swimming pool, a tennis court and a wellness centre. The water sports centre rents out canoes as well as diving and fishing equipment. At the *Bijoutier* restaurant there is always freshly caught fish on the menu. *Tel. 429 28 00 | www.alphonse-resort.com | Expensive*

The regional IDC airline flies from Mahé to the island once a week (flight time about 1 hour), and there are charter flights available on request. Flights can only be booked in conjunction with accommodation.

D'ARROS

(0) (*🗺 0*)

D'Arros lies 45km/28mi from Desroches and is best reached by boat (there are regular day trips to the island). The island – named after the marine commander Baron D'Arros – is worth a visit mainly for its diverse vegetation that covers an area of just half a square mile. Athough coconut palms grew here naturally, additional plantations were also laid out for the production of copra. The island was once owned by a nephew of the last Shah of Iran, who developed it for commercial use and promoted nature conservation but the island is now a nature reserve owned by the Save Our Seas Foundation. The environment has recovered well and the Wedge-tailed Shearwater (the chicks were considered a delicacy in the Seychelles) are now back from the brink of extinction.

DESROCHES

(0) (*🗺 0*)

The largest island of the Amirantes is about 230km/140mi from Mahé on an undersea basalt plateau. The island has a landing strip for the small island hopper of the IDC *(five times a week, flight time from Mahé 30 minutes)*. Desroches takes its name from a governor who ruled Mauritius in the 18th century. The island can be visited all year round but divers should limit themselves to the months of the north-west monsoon (Dec–March) as that is when there is clear underwater visibility. However, this is also the time that it is unfortunately not possible dive the steep wall at the outer edge of the lagoon – which drops thousands of feet into the depths of the Indian Ocean – due to extremely dangerous currents.

The sightseeing attractions of Desroches lie in almost equal parts above and below the water. On the island itself is the interesting and varied scenery and off its coast, the fascinating and colourful ★ *underwater world* with a myriad of tropical fish

CREOLE FOR TOURISTS

Of course you don't have to learn to speak Creole before you go on holiday – the staff in most of the hotels and restaurants speak English or French, often an additional foreign language (usually German or Italian). But you will be well prepared with a few Creole phrases. It also shows the locals that you are interested in their country.

Where can I find a restaurant? – *Kote i annan en restoran?*
Food/drinks – *Manze/bwar*
The menu, please – *Meni, silvouple*
A beer, please – *En labyer, silvouple*
A cup of coffee, please – *En Kafe, silvouple*
What kind of fish is that? – *Ki mannyer sa pwason i apele?*
Salt, sugar, bread, butter – *disel, disik, dipen, diber*
How much is it? – *Konbyen sa?*
The bill, please – *Bil, silvouple*
Where is the toilet? – *Kote i annan en kabinen, silvouple?*
My apologies! – *Ekskiz!*
No problem – *Pa dekwa*
Thank you! – *Mersi!*

and other marine life. Unfortunately some of the corals are still partly bleached. There are a number of hiking trails on the island, mostly lined with palm trees. A walk under the canopy of trees is ideal for observing the island's interesting INSIDER TIP **bird life** – in addition to the numerous other bird species, there are also common house sparrows, and no one knows quite how they got here.

Anyone looking for evening entertainment or even hustle and bustle will not find it in the Amirantes – nor on many of the other Seychelles islands. It is a far better idea to bring along a good book.

IDC flies to the island once a day from Mahé (the flight takes about 30 minutes), also charter flights by request. Flights can only be booked in conjunction with accommodation *(Desroches Island Lodge).*

Peace and quiet in beautiful surroundings: Desroches Island Lodge

The ★ *Desroches Island Lodge* is the only accommodation on the island, but offers its guests all the creature comforts (including a satellite telephone). The 20 rooms and 26 villas are located only a few feet from the beautiful, white sandy beach. There is a tennis court available for sporty guests. The only restaurant on the island *(Moderate)* also belongs to the hotel. Their speciality is delicious and surprisingly inexpensive fish dishes. *Tel. 422 90 03 | www.desroches-island.com | Moderate–Expensive*

POIVRE (0) *(0)*

Poivre Island is also called the island of spice; it was named after the French governor of Mauritius, Pierre Poivre. He has a place in history because he was the first to introduce and grow spices on the Seychelles. It is purely coincidence that *poivre* is the French word for pepper. Poivre is a rewarding destination throughout the year and there are some particularly appealing sailing cruises on offer (information available from tour operators in Victoria on Mahé).

TRIPS & TOURS

The tours are marked in green in the road atlas, the pull-out map and on the back cover

1 ROUND TRIP THROUGH THE SOUTH OF MAHÉ ISLAND

You should set aside a day for a leisurely round trip through the spectacular scenery of the southern part of Mahé Island. Of course there is also an opportunity to swim at one of the stunning beaches, particularly those at the southern tip of the island. As there are very few petrol stations on the main island, you should remember to fill up your car beforehand. The entire driving distance is about 60km/37mi and the tour begins and ends in Victoria. Maps are available at the bookstore at the Clock Tower in Mahé or at the hotel.

Make sure you set off early from Victoria, and head out towards the airport. From there you will take the coastal road to the south to the arts and crafts village of **Vilaz Artizanal** → p. 48. In front of an old wooden building in colonial style (which was once a popular restaurant) there are some small huts where the local artisans and craftsmen sell their products. In the main building there are three interesting rooms left in their original state and decorated with old furniture; admission is free. On the right of the approach road is a palm-thatched house, the *Maison de Coco*, which

Photo: The harbour bay in Victoria, Mahé

A round trip with plenty of variety on Mahé and a car hire and hiking combination through unspoilt nature on Praslin

houses a small exhibition of the equipment used to process coconuts as well as small gifts made from coconuts.

Only 2km/1.2mi further keep an eye out for the signpost for **La Marine** → p. 48. There is a workshop to the right of the main building where the locals craft beautiful models of historical boats. They are popular – if somewhat pricey – souvenirs from the Seychelles.

The trip continues to **Anse Royale**, which makes a wide curve along the road. Shortly after the small **Kaz Kreol** → p. 50 restaurant there is a signpost to the INSIDER TIP **Jardin du Roi** → p. 47 botanical gardens. There are four walks through the area, one of them through one of the last vestiges of tropical rainforest on Mahé. In an enclosure you will also find a few giant tortoises. The road trip still has a lot of attractions, so you shouldn't spend too long here.

The road then leads past **Anse Royale** and further along the coast before turning towards the interior of the island. At the beginning of **Quatre Bornes** turn immediately left at the roundabout and *Moderate)* that serves freshly caught seafood.

The second part of the round trip leads back to **Quatre Bornes** and from there down to **Takamaka** and **Baie Lazare**. Here you will find, right next to the *Quatre Bornes* police station, the small bistro

Anse Takamaka lies down in the south on the west coast of Mahé

continue to where the road forks after a mile or so: into *Intendance Road* and *Police Bay Road.*

Turning left takes you through a magnificent landscape of massive trees down to **Police Bay → p. 48**, one of the most beautiful bays in the Seychelles. Swimming here is just as dangerous as at **Anse Intendance → p. 47** due to the unpredictable currents. When you go right at the fork in the road you will reach Anse Intendance with the small restaurant INSIDER TIP *Jolie Rose (tel. 436 60 60 |* INSIDER TIP *Frangipani (daily 11am–8pm | tel. 441 34 54 | Budget)* serving refreshing drinks, light meals and delicious milkshakes in interesting flavours. Before you reach the picturesque Anse à la Mouche, one of the most gorgeous beaches in Mahé, you should consider a brief stop at the studio of well known painter **Michael Adams → p. 46**. Then the trip now leads back north, along the *West Coast Road* and on to **Anse à la Mouche**. Due to dangerous currents it is prohibited to swim at the beach that is right at the beginning of the road. But if you continue just a few hundred feet further you can unpack your swimsuit. If you want to end your afternoon here, there is the option to turn right at the school just after **Anse Louis** and to drive back towards Victoria (warning: the signpost is barely visible!). But then you will miss a further highlight of this trip. The route takes you via **Anse Boileau** and past **Grand' Anse** with the beautifully situated *Le Méridien Barbarons* hotel and to **Port Glaud**. A few kilometres after the village the road becomes narrow, which can become a test of patience when there is oncoming traffic. However, it runs through a fascinating landscape where the sea is right next to the road at one point and at others it is only visible deep down through dense forest. Just before where the road suddenly ends – because this area is a nature reserve – you will find the magnificent beach that forms the eastern edge of the **Port Launay Marine National Park**.

Back in **Port Glaud** and you need to be careful not to miss the turnoff to the left. The small sports field is a good way to orientate yourself. After you have gone past the last houses of Port Glaud the road winds its way uphill and leads past some pretty houses and on through an unspoilt landscape to the highest point at **Morne Blanc**, the third highest mountain on Mahé. Dense tea bushes line the road; the leaves are processed at the only tea factory in the Seychelles. If you are on the road at harvest time you can take a tour of the INSIDER TIP *Tea Factory (tel. 437 82 21)* if not, there is at least the opportunity to buy tea from the factory kiosk or at the restaurant.

Now the route heads downhill once again and it is only a few short miles to **Victoria**. When you see the sign on the left with the inscription *Historical Site – Mission Station*, then you should take your last break here. From the parking lot there is a path that leads past the crumbling remains of the ruins of a Jesuit mission station (destroyed by arson) and continues through a wide avenue of Dragon Blood Trees to a platform. From here you have a marvellous view of the verdant and pristine forests of the **Morne Seychellois National Park**.

The last stage is completed quickly. After driving through the valley with the beautiful name of **Val Riche** you will soon you reach the first houses of **Sans Souci** → **p. 34**, a wealthy suburb of Victoria. After Sans Souci comes **Bel Air** → **p. 34** with some equally pretty houses. The centre of the capital is then just a mile or so away.

HIKING ON PRASLIN

Praslin Island, with its many varied trails, is a good area for hikers and there are some particularly rewarding hiking trails in the Vallée de Mai National Park.

A simple, but very attractive hike leads through the **Vallée de Mai** → **p. 63**, where there are more than 6000 specimens of the legendary coco de mer palms. You should bank on at least one and a half hours for this walk, but you can make it shorter by simply turning around. You should at no time leave the signposted path! Another of the hikes in the Vallée du Mai National Park is the one that leads to **Glacis Noire**; it is quite challenging with a steep incline even though the entire route is only 3.5km/2mi long. Along the route there are specimens of all six palm species endemic to the Seychelles. Once you arrive at the top, you will have a fabulous view of the east coast of Praslin as well as the neighbouring islands (e.g. La Digue).

SPORTS & ACTIVITIES

There is far more to the Seychelles than the water sports so often associated with this travel destination.

Nonetheless, the recreational activities available are limited to a reasonable level in order not to put any unnecessary strain on the environment and the guests that are seeking peace and quiet. The larger hotels offer sports and fitness facilities such as tennis and squash.

CHARTER BOATS

It is well worth chartering a boat if you want to go fishing or diving. You can get information from several operators. The main providers are *VPM* and *Sunsail*. The central contact point on the Seychelles is the *Marine Charter Association (P.O. Box 204 | Victoria, Mahé | tel. 422 46 79 | mca@seychelles.net)*.

You can explore the Seychelles archipelago on your own with a sailing or motor yacht, a great alternative to a hotel room holiday. Day or weekly charters are available at *Azur Yachting Seychelles* on Eden Island *(tel. 424 25 16 or 271 91 21 | www.azuryachtingseychelles.com)*; also on Eden Island is the international charter operator *Moorings (www.moorings.com)* they offer a bareboat cruise but skippers with experience of the area can also be organised.

Photo: Snorkelling off Praslin

The crystal clear water and beautiful marine world of the Indian Ocean make the islands a popular choice for divers and snorkellers

Luxury catamarans with full crew are available from *Elegant Yachting (Eden Island | tel. 451 57 36 | www.elegant-yachting.com)*.

CYCLING

Whilst bicycles on Mahé are not an ideal mode of transport (the streets are congested and there are no designated cycling trails) on La Digue and Praslin the bicycle is part of daily life for locals as well as tourists. Rentals are available on La Digue at the harbour and on Praslin at Côte d'Or and Grand' Anse.

FISHING

The rich fishing grounds of the Seychelles are very attractive to fishermen. On the beaches of the main islands there are numerous well established boat rental companies that offer half or full day fishing trips. The costs lie between 5000 rupees (half day) and 17,000 rupees (full day), depending on the type of boat and the equipment. The waters off Bird and Denis Islands are fabulous for fishing as this is where the seabed drops off more than 1800m/6000ft. The Alphonse, Desroches and North Islands are popular with fly fishermen *(info: www.seyfly.sc)*. For coastal fishing the best areas are the lagoons and cliffs on the south coast of Mahé and no fishing permits are necessary. In April and October fishing competitions are held on the Seychelles.

Challenging course, unbeatable views: the Lémuria Resort golf course on Praslin

GOLF

The Seychelles only became an attractive travel destination for golfers after the opening of an ● 18 hole course in the north of Praslin (Anse Kerlan), prior to that the small 9 hole course at the *Reef Hotel (Anse aux Pins | tel. 4376252)* on Mahé was the only option available. The 18 hole course has some spectacular views of the world's most beautiful beaches. The course is also open to non-guests of the hotel through the *Lémuria Resort (tel. 4281281)*.

HIKING

When the weather is not good for swimming you can take some time to get to know the islands from another perspective, by going on some hikes through the scenic and varied countryside. There are a few hikes detailed in the section on Mahé but you can do a hike on just about every island as there are no dangerous animals to worry about. You will need some sturdy walking shoes and bear in mind that even the designated trails may be partially overgrown. However, the authorities have promised that the most important trails on Mahé will be well-maintained in the future.

HORSEBACK RIDING

A INSIDER TIP beach ride on an Arabian horse is also possible for less experienced riders. On the main island of Mahé you can try the *Utegangar Riding Centre (at the Le Meridien Barbarons Hotel | daily 8am–6pm | tel. 471 23 55 | www.utegangar.no/seychelleneeng.htm)*. On La Digue you can go riding on *L'Union Estate (daily 8am–3pm | tel. 42 34 40)* near Cliff Ladouceur. For both riding centres it is recommended that you first make a telephonic reservation.

SCUBA DIVING & SNORKELLING

The Seychelles is one of the most beautiful diving sites on earth. The best times are the months at the turn of the monsoon, April/May and Oct/Nov, when the sea is calm and clear. There are diving centres at almost all the larger hotels. An individual dive costs about 700 rupees (without equipment) but they also offer dives with equipment as well as nitrox diving. A PADI diving course costs 6000 rupees. A rather unique attraction is a INSIDER TIP dive with some large (but harmless) whale sharks, they can be found in the waters between October and April. *Seychelles Underwater Centre | P. O. Box 384 | tel. 434 54 45 | www.diveseychelles.com.sc*

The following waters are ideal for snorkelling: the Ste Anne and Port Launay National Parks off Mahé, off Côte d'Or and Anse Lazio on Praslin, as well as the area off the smaller island around Praslin (such as St Pierre) and off the west coast of La Digue. If you haven't brought your own equipment, you can rent it on site.

SURFING

The Seychelles is only suitable for surfing under certain conditions. Some good surfing spots on Mahé that work in the middle of the year are *Anse aux Poules Bleues* and *Carana Beach* while *Grand' Anse* and *Soleil d'Or* are good at the end of the year; also, depending on weather conditions, *Anse Kerlan* on Praslin and *Grand' Anse* on La Digue.

SWIMMING

While most of the waters off the Seychelles are safe not all of the beaches on are suitable for swimming. The beaches with dangerous and unpredictable currents always have multilingual signs warning of the dangers. A far less dangerous obstacle whilst swimming is that some beaches are so shallow during some seasons that the water barely covers your feet. Good swimming beaches on Mahé are the popular *Beau Vallon Bay*, *Anse à la Mouche* (with its protective coral reef) and the scenic *Anse Intendance* (strong breakers sometimes). On Praslin there is the endless *Anse Volbert* which is best from May to September. The granite boulders that frame *Anse la Source à Jean* offer a beautiful background for swimming and sun bathing. Equally attractive are the beaches on the east coast of La Digue *(Grand' Anse, Petite Anse, Anse Cocos)*, which are however, not protected by reefs.

WATER SPORTS

The water sports centres are along the bay of *Beau Vallon* on Mahé and the *Côte d'Or* on Praslin. Most of the accommodation on the Outer Islands also have their own water sports centres. Facilities include jet-skiing, kayaking, waterskiing and parasailing.

TRAVEL WITH KIDS

The Seychelles are not only ideal for a holiday but also a paradise for children – not least because it is one of the few countries in the tropics that doesn't require additional vaccinations and where there are practically no dangerous animals and plants.

The Seychelles are a family-friendly holiday destination and if you are travelling with your offspring the locals may approach for a friendly chat, with the older ones often patting the children on their heads. This is a common gesture and is just their way of showing how much they like children. You won't find people frowning at you if your child behaves the way children behave, by playing loudly or kicking up a fuss.

The one danger to children is the harsh, equatorial sun and even the lush vegetation offers little in the way of protection from its rays. If you have taken the necessary precautions (a hat and a tee shirt even while swimming!) then the endless, sandy beaches are an absolute pleasure. The bight sand is fine, powdery and usually very clean. In many places the beaches have very shallow waters that are ideal for children but you should always be on the lookout for the waves and take the signposted warnings very seriously. It is also a good idea to have beach sandals with non-slip soles as some of the beaches have sharp-edged corals that can cause nasty injuries.

When choosing your accommodation, it is worth noting that some hotels have locations that are not suitable for children – such as the *Sunset Beach Hotel* on Mahé, which is on a rocky outcrop right on the sea. These hotels usually have a prescribed minimum age for their guests. On the other hand, some large hotels offer special entertainment programmes for their younger guests as well as a babysitter service for those parents who need some time alone. Some hotels also offer family suites, most have cots available for infants and many hotels have space for an extra bed for an older child. If children want their own rooms, larger hotels have adjacent rooms with connecting doors. Travel agencies usually indicate these options in their catalogues.

The high-end category of hotels also have offers especially geared to the needs of

An endless sandpit, animals to pet, tea and coconut harvests – the Seychelles is more nature park than an amusement park

children such as the *Lémuria Resort,* which attracted so many children that, in addition to the children's playground, they now also have options for older children and teenagers. There are even spas with treatments for children and teenagers so they can enjoy a yoga class or even a chocolate massage!

On Mahé it is worth taking the children on a visit to the *Botanical Gardens (→ p. 34)* and older children will enjoy exploring the *Jardin du Roi (→ p. 47)* where you can explain to them where spices come from, which most only know in their processed form in their kitchen cupboards. The same goes for the *Tea Factory (→ p. 40)* on Mahé, where they can experience the growing, harvesting and processing of tea, while the *L'Union Estate (→ p. 58)* on La Digue demonstrates the processing of coconuts. If you are staying on Praslin, you should book a day trip by boat to the neighbouring islands of Cousin and Curieuse, where you are guaranteed to INSIDER TIP encounter giant tortoises and all kinds of exotic birds and the tortoises don't mind if you pet them.

Even though a minimum age of 12 years is mandatory for participation in the dive courses, the underwater world need not be denied to younger children. From 8 years of age they can participate in a *Bubblemaker* course where they learn how to use a mask and snorkel. Those 12 years and older can do the *Junior PADI Open Water Diver Certificate.* It is important to remember that your children need to obtain a diving medical certificate from a sports physician prior to departure.

Glass bottom boat trips are available on Mahé and other islands. Without getting your feet wet, you can observe corals, fish and other marine creatures up close.

FESTIVALS & EVENTS

There are a thousand reasons to celebrate: this is the motto that the residents of the Seychelles live and work by and their positive attitude towards life is very contagious. One such expression of their zest for life is the Sega, a dance whose origin is clearly found in nearby Africa. The genuine Sega can however only be seen on the more remote islands. A modern version with the latest disco rhythms is danced in the clubs on Mahé. Then there are the Kamtole dances, which have a lot in common with the American Square Dance and the Scottish Reel, but actually come from France, where they were called Contredanse. The dance has a so-called *commander* who calls out which steps are danced. Another popular dance is the Moutia, which was originally the songs of slaves. The dance received a bad reputation, because – particularly in the eyes of the clergy – the movements were sometimes suggestive and lewd. The Moutia is usually spontaneously danced at night under an open sky. The goatskin drums are first warmed and stretched at a fire and the firelight makes the dancers and their movements seem shrouded in an almost ghostly light.

PUBLIC HOLIDAYS

1/2 Jan *New Year's Day;* **Good Friday**; **1 May** *Workers Day;* **Corpus Christi**; **5 June** *Liberation Day*; **18 June** *National Day;* **29 June** *Independence Day;* **15 Aug** *Assumption Day;* **1 Nov** *All Saints Day;* **8 Dec** *Immaculate Conception;* **25 Dec** *Christmas Day*

When a public holiday falls on a Sunday, the Monday following it is a holiday.

FESTIVALS

You can rely on the fact that there will always be ▶ INSIDER TIP ***spontaneous street festivals*** somewhere on one of the islands, in one of the villages.

Even ▶● ***going to church on Sunday*** becomes a festival, perhaps because there isn't much variety during the week. The well dressed churchgoers all file out to church. Since almost all inhabitants of the Seychelles are Catholic, the various church festivals also play a particularly important role.

There are solemn ▶★ ***processions*** on Assumption Day; the inhabitants of La

Pure joie de vivre: the Seychellois are a happy folk – even the Sunday church service is a very festive occasion

Digue are particularly famous for their picturesque processions.

The ▶ ***anniversary of the coup d'état*** on 5 June and the ▶ ***Independence Day*** on 29 June – are both celebrated with parades in Victoria on Mahé and with various other festivities (sport competitions, children's festivals etc).

EVENTS

The most significant festival on the Seychelles is the ▶★ ***Carnival International***, which attracts thousands of visitors to Victoria on the first weekend in March every year. The highlight is the colourful procession with a float that commemorates the first settlement on the Seychelles. Carnival groups are invited from all over the world.

Every year in October the week long ▶★ ***Festival Kreol*** takes place on Mahé with traditional dances and Creole music. The festival combines folklore with serious academic research (mainly by the *Lenstiti Kreol* research Anse aux Pins). Further highlights are the music show *Lakadans*, fashion shows *(Defile Lanmod)* and the Sunday at the sea *(Dimans Kreol Bor Lanmer)* on Beau Vallon beach on Mahé.

In honour of the Hindu elephant god ▶ ***Vinayagar*** a large festival takes place every year in September in the Arulmikunavasakkthi Temple in Victoria. And in October there is also a Hindu ▶ ***Deepavali Festival*** in honour of the Hindu goddess Lakshmi.

The ▶ INSIDER TIP ***SUBIOS* Underwater Festival** (Oct/Nov) combines diving and snorkelling during the day with slide shows, film and video presentations and other events in various hotels in the evening. Information: *www.subios.com*

LINKS, BLOGS, APPS & MORE

LINKS

▶ www.seychelles.travel The official website of the Seychelles Tourist Board. Very informative site, nicely done and well maintained. Lots of information about the island's nature, climate, itinerary ideas, events and an interactive gallery and videos

▶ www.virtualseychelles.sc Information and current events on Seychelles and four webcams that update every 15 seconds

▶ www.experienceseychelles.com A comprehensive online guide. The site offers accommodation options, suggestions for excursions, nature trails, charters and the like. The gallery tab has videos and slide shows.

▶ www.seychelles-hotels.org Full range of accommodation options from private villas to luxury resorts also dive and yacht charter information

▶ www.natureseychelles.org An excellent site for those interested in the conservation activities on the Seychelles

BLOGS & FORUMS

▶ www.lonelyplanet.com/thorntree Forum to exchange travel information and ask advice. After your trip, you can post your own evaluations, photos and reports

▶ www.tripwolf.com Travel tips, activities, photos, blogs and evaluations from the travel community. Background reports and the possibility of direct bookings for accommodation

PHOTOS & VIDEOS

▶ www.youtube.com/watch?v=OIcNpUW1oxA A taste of paradise, this video touches on the geography, history and culture of the Seychelles

▶ www.youtube.com/watch?v=4AHkKYUKiHQ&feature=related Video impressions of the colourful culture of the Seychelles, with a section about the

Regardless of whether you are still preparing your trip or already on the Seychelles: these addresses will provide you with more information, videos and networks to make your holiday even more enjoyable

annual *Creole Festival* celebration that takes place in October

PHOTOS & VIDEOS

▶ www.youtube.com/watch?v=YhtBt7CCc3U&feature=related A video by the *Seychelles Tourist Board* with fantastic shots of the beaches, dive sites, wildlife, landscape and other sightseeing attractions on the Seychelles

▶ www.youtube.com/watch?v=HdibaJMnuVs Beautifully shot video showcasing Mahé, Praslin and La Digue's beaches

▶ www.youtube.com/watch?v=4QwyGGyAro8 North Island – Barefoot Luxury, the title says it all. A video about the beautiful, tropical island with some shots of the luxurious accommodation on offer as well as the local fauna, flora and underwater world

▶ www.youtube.com/watch?v=BgtDDspdXVc Great video about all the excellent dive opportunities offered by the underwater world of the Seychelles, with detailed dive information

APPS

▶ Seychelles Islands Free App guide to the Seychelles with many current events, useful info, news, weather forecasts and GPS-supported maps

▶ Seychelles Islands Travel Guide – Mobile Travel App with photos, info, maps (GPS), search function that serves as a complete travel planning tool

▶ Seychelles GPS Map Navigator App by Flytomap is an offline navigation app with maps (GPS) and satellite pictures to navigate throughout the country and plan your trip

NETWORK

▶ www.seychellesweekly.com Weekly online newspaper with, sports and cultural events, news, politics and the weather

▶ twitter.com/Seychelles_org Twitter account by So Seychelles with regular information about nature conservation, travel news and images and also retweets from the tourism board

TRAVEL TIPS

ARRIVAL

The Seychelles are serviced by national lines such as *Air Seychelles (www.airseychelles.net)* and *British Airways (www.britishairways.com)* as well as via European hubs such as Amsterdam or Paris. The flight from London to Mahé takes about 10 hours. There are also flights via the Gulf with airlines such as *Qatar Airways (www.qatarairways.com)* or *Emirates (www.emirates.com/uk)* via Dubai.

The Seychelles International Airport on Mahé, where all commercial aircraft arrive from abroad, lies in the centre of the island on the east coast. Almost every place on Mahé is within an hour's taxi ride from here. When flying onward to other Seychelles islands you need to take into account the luggage weight restrictions (10–15kg/22–33lbs) as you will be charged if your luggage is overweight. Air Seychelles has connecting flights to Alphonse, Bird, Denis, Desroches, Frégate and North Islands, but these flights are treated as charter flights and need to be booked by the your travel operator.

RESPONSIBLE TRAVEL

It doesn't take a lot to be environmentally friendly whilst travelling. Don't just think about your carbon footprint whilst flying to and from your holiday destination but also about how you can protect nature and culture abroad. As a tourist it is especially important to respect nature, look out for local products, cycle instead of driving, save water and much more. If you would like to find out more about eco-tourism please visit: *www.ecotourism.org*

BANKS & CURRENCY EXCHANGE

The import and export of local currency is unlimited. Foreign currency can be brought in, but only to the amount declared on the customs form. You should change money only at authorised centres! There are several banks in the capital Victoria *(Mon–Fri usually 8am–2pm, Sat 8am–11am)* and there are airport exchange counters that are open when flights depart or arrive. You can also change money at your hotel reception, however, the rate will be considerably worse. The exchange of Seychellios currency is only done on presentation of your original exchange receipt so remember to hold on to your receipt! Cash or traveller's cheques in euro or US dollars are accepted in hotels and with tour organisers. Bills in hotel restaurants and for tourist services can also be paid in (officially exchanged) local currency and you will need local cash for small purchases and if you want to take a taxi. All major credit cards are widely accepted and can be used to pay for hotel, restaurant and hire car services all of which will be charged for in foreign currency. Some of the larger shops and hotel boutiques also accept credit cards. Cards can also be used for making cash withdrawals and there are ATMs at banks on the main islands and at the airport. Cash drawn will be in rupees.

CAR HIRE

You can rent a car on Mahé and Praslin (minimum age 21 years) on presentation

Holiday from start to finish: the most important addresses and information for your trip to the Seychelles

of your national driver's licence (drive on the left). The vehicle can be delivered to your hotel, but there are also plenty of rental companies at the airport. The network of petrol stations on Mahé was expanded in recent years, however, they have different opening hours (usually 9am–5pm). There are numerous car rental companies and it is worth comparing prices. Remember to document any previous damages to the car when you take over the vehicle. You can expect to pay about 1000 rupees per day excluding petrol.

The road network on Mahé and Praslin is well developed, but the roads often lack a guard rail, something that can be quite dangerous as the side of the road often falls off sharply and if you swerve you can land in the ditch off the road. Maximum speed in town 40km/h (25mph), out of town 65km/h (40mph).

CURRENCY CONVERTER

£	SCR	SCR	£
1	20	10	0.50
3	60	30	1.50
5	100	50	2.50
13	260	130	6.50
40	800	400	20
75	1,500	750	37.50
120	2,400	1,200	60
250	5,000	2,500	125
500	10,000	5,000	250

$	SCR	SCR	$
1	12.50	10	0.80
3	37.50	30	2.40
5	62.50	50	4
13	163	130	10.50
40	500	400	32
75	940	750	60
120	1,500	1,200	97
250	3,125	2,500	200
500	6,250	5,000	400

For current exchange rates see www.xe.com

CONSULATES & EMBASSIES

BRITISH HIGH COMMISSION

3nd Floor, Oliaji Trade Centre | Francis Rachel Street | Victoria | Mahé | Tel. +248 428 36 66 | bhcvictoria@fco.gov.uk

CONSULAR AGENCY OF THE UNITED STATES OF AMERICA

Suite 23, 2nd Floor, Oliaji Trade Centre | Francis Rachel Street | Victoria | Mahé | Tel. +248 22 22 56 | usoffice@seychelles.net

CUSTOMS

Your duty free allowance includes the import of 200 cigarettes, 2L of spirits and 2L wine as well as items intended for your personal consumption. Allowance is also made for cameras, personal electronic equipment and sporting equipment. Weapons (including spear guns) and ammunition are strictly prohibited. Seychelles also has strict bio-security measures in place to prevent any threats to the environment and as such it is prohibited to import any seeds, plants, animal products, tea and the likes. Drugs and all forms of pornography are forbidden.

You may not export tortoise shells and corals and written permission is required to export coco de mer (available from authorised sellers). The following goods can be exported duty-free when you leave the Seychelles: 200 cigarettes or 50 cigars or 250g tobacco, 1L of spirits or 4L wine, 250g coffee and other goods up to a value of £340/€430. Travellers to the US who are residents of the country do not have to pay duty on articles purchased overseas up to the value of $800, but there are limits on the amount of alcoholic beverages and tobacco products. For the regulations for international travel for US residents please see *www.cbp.gov*.

ELECTRICITY

The voltage is 240 volt AC 50 Hz. The standard plugs are British three pin so visitors from other countries will need an adaptor and voltage converter which you can get at the hotel reception or in shops in Victoria.

EMERGENCY SERVICES

Police, fire brigade, doctor and ambulance: *tel. 999*

HEALTH

On Mahé, La Digue, Praslin and Silhouette there are well equipped hospitals. In the hospital on Mahé *(Mont Fleuri | tel. 422 44 00, 438 80 00)* complicated operations are possible, and there is also a 24-hour emergency service. For all islands the emergency number is *999*. Whilst locals are treated in hospital for free, foreign visitors have to pay for treatment so travel insurance is advisable, which includes a return flight should it be required. There are pharmacies on all inhabited islands.

IMMIGRATION

At arrivals you need a passport which is valid at least until the day of the scheduled departure, a valid return or onward ticket and sufficient funds for accommodation. Package tourists do not require such documentation. On arrival you are given a visitor's permit, which is valid for a month and can be extended during this time at the *Department of Immigration (Mahé | Independence House | tel. +24 84 29 36 36 | info@immigration.gov.sc)* for up to nine months. Children require a children's passport with photograph. There is no longer a passenger service charge, it is now included in the fare.

INFORMATION

SEYCHELLES TOURIST OFFICE UK

11 Grosvenor Crescent, Fourth Floor | London, SW1X 7EE | tel. +44 (0) 20 72 45 06 80 | info-tourism.uk@seychelles.travel | www.seychelles.travel | Mon–Fri 9am–5pm

LOCAL SEYCHELLES TOURIST OFFICE

- *Mahé | Independence House | Victoria | Mahé | tel. 461 08 00/-03/-04/-05 | info@seychelles.net | Mon–Fri 8am–4.30pm, Sat 9am–midday, closed Sundays*
- *La Digue | La Passe | tel. 423 43 93 | stbladigue@seychelles.com | Mon–Fri 8am–5pm, Sat 9am–midday, public holidays 9am–midday, closed Sundays*
- *Praslin | Îles des Palmes Airport, Grand' Anse | tel. 423 33 46 | stbpraslin@seychelles.sc | Mon–Fri 8am–4pm, Sat 8am–midday, public holidays 8am–midday, closed Sundays*
- *Baie Ste Anne | Praslin | Jetty | tel. 423 26 69 | stbpraslin@seychelles.net | Mon–Fri 8am–4pm, Sat 8am–midday, public holidays 8am–midday, closed Sundays*

INTERNET CAFÉS & WI-FI

On the Seychelles there are three Internet service providers, which each have an

Internet café in Victoria (approx. 35 rupees 15 min):

- *Doubleclick Seychelles | Maison la Rosière | Victoria | tel. 422 47 96 | doubleclicksey@gmail.com*
- *Incipe Seychelles | 6&7 MS Complex | Revolution Avenue | Victoria | tel. 426 66 99 | office@incipe.com*
- *Kokonet Café | Pirates Arms Building | Independence Avenue | Victoria | tel. 447 47 47 | kokonet@seychelles.sc*

There are other Internet cafés on Praslin and La Digue. The more expensive hotels offer their guests either PCs with Internet connection or Wi-Fi hotspots with connection in your room or areas like the hotel reception, lobby or bar. However, the speed is slow and broadband is not yet available in the Seychelles.

PHONE & MOBILE PHONE

Dialling codes: *Seychelles: +248 | UK: +44 | USA: +1*. In the Seychelles, there are no codes for the individual islands or towns.

The Seychelles are connected via satellite to almost all other countries and you can make direct calls from hotels and from the public pay phones. Calls from hotels are expensive, it is cheaper from public telephones. Phone cards are available at the main post office, in many shops on Mahé or at telephone companies such as *Airtel* and *Cable & Wireless Ltd.* For pay phones with coins you need 1 and 5 rupee coins.

Mobile phone owners can use their mobile phones in Seychelles if you activate roaming and connect to the local network but this is quite an expensive option. It is cheaper to get a prepaid card; starter packs cost approx. 700 rupees including a credit balance. But you will only be able to use it to call Seychelles numbers.

POST

The main post office is in Victoria on Independence Avenue, opposite the Clock Tower *(Mon–Fri 8am–4pm, Sat 8am–midday)*. On Praslin there are post offices in Baie Ste Anne and Grande Anse Village *(Mon–Fri 8am–midday, 2pm–4pm, Sat 8am–midday)*. Mailboxes are found in even the smaller towns, but you can also hand in your post at the hotel.

BUDGETING

Lemonade	£2.50/$3.50 *for a shop bought bottle*
Coco de mer	£130–260/$200–400 *for a legally exportable coco de mer*
Wine	£20/$30 *for a bottle in a restaurant*
Hire car	from £30/$45 *a day*
Pizza	£5/$7 *at the Pirates Arms Restaurant in Victoria*
Day trip	from £90/$130 *to a neighbouring island incl. transfer and a meal*

PRICES & CURRENCY

The Seychelles currency is the rupee (Seychelles Rupee, SCR). 100 cents is 1 rupee. Bank notes are available in 10, 20, 25, 50, 100 and 500, coins in 1, 5, 10 and 25 cents and 1 and 5 rupees. Restaurant, petrol and taxi fares are on par with those in Europe but bus fares are cheaper. Alcohol, tobacco and luxury goods are expensive. Since a change in the exchange control regulations, services (e.g. entrance fees) can be paid in Seychelles rupee (SCR).

Cousin Island with exclusive Cousine Island in the distance

PUBLIC TRANSPORT

Buses depart from Victoria for almost all parts of the main island of Mahé; the central bus station is located on Palm Street opposite Unity House. Although there are official timetables, they are seldom reliable. At bus stops outside Victoria you should stand on the side of the road and wave to get the driver's attention. There are also buses on Praslin that run daily between 5.30am–10pm, after 6.30pm not as regularly though.
Taxis are only available on Mahé and Praslin, the prices are similar to what you would pay in Europe. The drivers often speak enough English to understand the destination. Make sure the taxi meter is switched on. There are *ferries* that commute to Praslin and La Digue several times a day from Inter Island Quay on Mahé. Bookings for the ferry from Praslin to La Digue are via *Inter Island Ferry Service (tel. 423 23 29/ www.seychelles.net/iif)*. The high speed catamaran 'Cat Cocos' commutes between Mahé and Praslin *(approx. 60 min)* up to three times a day from a terminal on Eden Island, off Mahé over a bridge. Bookings are made via hotel reception or *tel. 432 48 43* or email: reservation@catcocos.com. A real experience is the passage from Mahé to La Digue with the schooner 'La Belle Seraphina' that carries cargo as well as passengers *(tel. 251 13 45)*.
Air Seychelles has *flights* between Mahé and other islands. It is advisable to book well in advance, especially in high season when the flights are often fully booked. The small aircraft are not suitable for large luggage and there is usually a limit of 10kg/22lbs *(Air Seychelles | Victoria | tel. 439 10 00)*.
Another excellent option (not exactly cheap) is to do a transfer in a helicopter with *Helicopter Seychelles (www.helicopterseychelles.sc)* which will give you wonderful views of the islands. The cost for a flight with up to eight people (60 min) is about 20,000 rupees.

TIME

The Seychelles is 4 hours ahead of GMT, 3 hours ahead of UK summer time and 2 hours ahead of CET summer time.

TIPPING

Tipping is not obligatory in the Seychelles, however, waiters, taxi drivers and hotel staff all welcome tips.

WHAT TO WEAR

Due to the constant warm temperatures, light summery clothes (such as breathable and easy to wash cottons) can be worn throughout the year. Beach sandals are important as there are sharp corals. Upmarket hotels and restaurants have a dress code and shorts and tee shirts are not an option. It is also a good idea to take a good sun hat, sunglasses with UV protection and plenty of sun screen and insect repellent. There are lots of easy walks and hikes so if you plan to walk then you should have some sturdy walking shoes, travel binoculars and a lightweight windcheater.

WEATHER, WHEN TO GO

The daytime temperatures are usually between 24°C/75°F and 33°C/90°F throughout the year. May to October are recommended, and then there is a chance of some overcast days. Most rainfall occurs in December and January, and the driest months are June, July and August.

Ideal conditions for snorkelling, swimming and scuba diving are usually found in April and May and October and November, when the sea is calm, the water very warm and visibility is excellent. The bird breeding season is also in April while the best time for surfing and windsurfing is from May to September. During peak holiday season (over Easter, December to January and July to August) hotel prices increase substantially and finding accommodation can be a struggle.

WEATHER ON THE SEYCHELLES

	Jan	Feb	March	April	May	June	July	Aug	Sept	Oct	Nov	Dec
Daytime temperatures in °C/°F	28/82	29/84	29/84	30/86	29/84	28/82	27/81	27/81	28/82	28/82	29/84	28/82
Nighttime temperatures in °C/°F	24/75	25/77	25/77	25/77	25/77	25/77	24/75	24/75	24/75	24/75	24/75	24/75
Sunshine hours/day	6	6	7	8	8	7	7	7	7	7	7	7
Precipitation days/month	15	10	11	10	9	9	8	7	8	9	12	15
Water temperatures in °C/°F	27/81	28/82	28/82	29/84	28/82	27/81	26/79	26/79	26/79	26/79	27/81	27/81

USEFUL PHRASES FRENCH

IN BRIEF

Yes/No/Maybe	oui/non/peut-être
Please/Thank you	s'il vous plaît/merci
Good morning!/afternoon!/ evening!/night!	Bonjour!/Bonjour!/ Bonsoir!/Bonne nuit!
Hello!/goodbye!/See you!	Salut!/Au revoir!/Salut!
Excuse me, please	Pardon!
My name is ...	Je m'appelle ...
I'm from ...	Je suis de ...
May I ...?/ Pardon?	Puis-je ...?/Comment?
I would like to .../ have you got ...?	Je voudrais .../ Avez-vous?
How much is ...?	Combien coûte ...?
I (don't) like this	Ça (ne) me plaît (pas).
good/bad/broken	bon/mauvais/cassé
too much/much/little	trop/beaucoup/peu
all/nothing	tout/rien
Help!/Attention!	Au secours/attention
police/fire brigade/ ambulance	police/pompiers/ ambulance
Could you please help me?	Est-ce que vous pourriez m'aider?
Do you speak English?	Parlez-vous anglais?
Do you understand?	Est-ce que vous comprenez?
Could you please ...?	Pourriez vous ... s'il vous plait?
... repeat that	répéter
... speak more slowly	parler plus lentement
... write that down	l'écrire

DATE & TIME

Monday/Tuesday	lundi/mardi
Wednesday/Thursday	mercredi/jeudi
Friday/Saturday/ Sunday	vendredi/samedi/ dimanche
working day/holiday	jour ouvrable/jour férié
today/tomorrow/ yesterday	aujourd'hui /demain/ hier
hour/minute	heure/minute
day/night/week	jour/nuit/semaine
month/year	mois/année
What time is it?	Quelle heure est-t-il?

Tu parles français?

"Do you speak French?" This guide will help you to say the basic words and phrases in French

It's three o'clock	Il est trois heures
It's half past three.	Il est trois heures et demi
a quarter to four	quatre heures moins le quart

TRAVEL

open/closed	ouvert/fermé
entrance/exit	entrée/sortie
departure/arrival	départ/arrivée
toilets/restrooms / ladies/gentlemen	toilettes/ femmes/hommes
(no) drinking water	eau (non) potable
Where is ...?/Where are ...?	Où est ...?/Où sont ...?
left/right	à gauche/à droite
straight ahead/back	tout droit/en arrière
close/far	près/loin
bus/tram/underground / taxi/cab	bus/tramway/métro/taxi
stop/cab stand	arrêt/station de taxi
parking lot/parking garage	parking
street map/map	plan de ville/carte routière
train station/harbour/ airport	gare/port/ aéroport
schedule/ticket	horaire/billet
single/return	aller simple/aller-retour
train/track/platform	train/voie/quai
I would like to rent ... a car/a bicycle/ a boat	Je voudrais ... louer une voiture/un vélo/ un bateau
petrol/gas station	station d'essence
petrol/gas / diesel	essence/diesel
breakdown/repair shop	panne/garage

FOOD & DRINK

The menu, please	La carte, s'il vous plaît
Could I please have ...?	Puis-je avoir ... s'il vous plaît
bottle/carafe/glass	bouteille/carafe/verre
knife/fork/spoon	couteau/fourchette/cuillère
salt/pepper/sugar	sel/poivre/sucre
vinegar/oil	vinaigre/huile
milk/cream/lemon	lait/crême/citron
cold/too salty/not cooked	froid/trop salé/pas cuit

with/without ice/sparkling	avec/sans glaçons/gaz
vegetarian	végétarien(ne)
May I have the bill, please	Je voudrais payer, s'il vous plaît
bill	addition

SHOPPING

pharmacy/chemist	pharmacie/droguerie
baker/market	boulangerie/marché
shopping centre	centre commercial
department store	grand magasin
100 grammes/1 kilo	cent grammes/un kilo
expensive/cheap/price	cher/bon marché/prix
more/less	plus/moins
organically grown	de l'agriculture biologique

ACCOMMODATION

I have booked a room	J'ai réservé une chambre
Do you have any ... left?	Avez-vous encore ...?
single room/double room	chambre simple/double
breakfast	petit déjeuner
half board/ full board (American plan)	demi-pension/ pension complète
shower/sit-down bath	douche/bain
balcony/terrace	balcon /terrasse
key/room card	clé/carte magnétique
luggage/suitcase/bag	bagages/valise/sac

BANKS, MONEY & CREDIT CARDS

bank/ATM/pin code	banque/guichet automatique/code
cash/credit card	comptant/carte de crédit
bill/coin	billet/monnaie

HEALTH

doctor/dentist/ paediatrician	médecin/dentiste/ pédiatre
hospital/emergency clinic	hôpital/urgences
fever/pain	fièvre/douleurs
diarrhoea/nausea	diarrhée/nausée
sunburn	coup de soleil
inflamed/injured	enflammé/blessé
plaster/bandage	pansement/bandage
ointment/pain reliever	pommade/analgésique

POST, TELECOMMUNICATIONS & MEDIA

stamp	timbre
letter/postcard	lettre/carte postale
I need a landline phone card	J'ai besoin d'une carte téléphonique pour fixe.
I'm looking for a prepaid card for my mobile	Je cherche une recharge pour mon portable.
Where can I find internet access?	Où puis-je trouver un accès à internet?
dial/connection/engaged	composer/connection/occupé
socket/charger	prise électrique/chargeur
computer/battery/rechargeable battery	ordinateur/batterie/ accumulateur
at sign (@)	arobase
internet address (URL)/ e-mail address	adresse internet/ mail
internet connection/wi-fi	accès internet/wi-fi
e-mail/file/print	mail/fichier/imprimer

LEISURE, SPORTS & BEACH

beach	plage
sunshade/lounger	parasol/transat
low tide/high tide/current	marée basse/marée haute/courant
cable car/chair lift	téléphérique/télésiège
(rescue) hut	refuge

NUMBERS

0	zéro	17	dix-sept
1	un, une	18	dix-huite
2	deux	19	dix-neuf
3	trois	20	vingt
4	quatre	30	trente
5	cinq	40	quarante
6	six	50	cinquante
7	sept	60	soixante
8	huit	70	soixante-dix
9	neuf	80	quatre-vingt
10	dix	90	quatre-vingt-dix
11	onze	100	cent
12	douze	200	deux cents
13	treize	1000	mille
14	quatorze		
15	quinze	½	un[e] demi[e]
16	seize	¼	un quart

NOTES
www.marco-polo.com

MARCO POLO TRAVEL GUIDES

ALGARVE
AMSTERDAM
ATHENS
AUSTRALIA
BANGKOK
BARCELONA
BERLIN
BRAZIL
BRUSSELS
BUDAPEST
BULGARIA
CALIFORNIA
CAMBODIA
CAPE TOWN
WINE LANDS, GARDEN ROUTE
CAPE VERDE
CHINA
COLOGNE
COPENHAGEN
CORFU
COSTA BLANCA
VALENCIA
COSTA DEL SOL
GRANADA
CRETE
CUBA
CYPRUS
NORTH AND SOUTH
DUBAI
DUBLIN
DUBROVNIK & DALMATIAN COAST
EDINBURGH
EGYPT
EGYPT'S RED SEA RESORTS
FINLAND
FLORENCE
FLORIDA
FRENCH ATLANTIC COAST
FRENCH RIVIERA
NICE, CANNES & MONACO
FUERTEVENTURA
GRAN CANARIA
GREECE
HONG KONG
MACAU
ICELAND
INDIA
INDIA SOUTH
GOA & KERALA
IRELAND
ISRAEL
ISTANBUL
JORDAN
KOS
KRAKOW
LAKE GARDA
LANZAROTE
LAS VEGAS
LISBON
LONDON
LOS ANGELES
MADEIRA
PORTO SANTO
MADRID
MALLORCA
MALTA
GOZO
MAURITIUS
MILAN
MOROCCO
MUNICH
NAPLES & THE AMALFI COAST
NEW YORK
NEW ZEALAND
NORWAY
OSLO
PARIS
PHUKET
PORTUGAL
PRAGUE
RHODES
ROME
SAN FRANCISCO
SARDINIA
SCOTLAND
SEYCHELLES
SHANGHAI
SICILY
SINGAPORE
SOUTH AFRICA
STOCKHOLM
TENERIFE
THAILAND
TURKEY
TURKEY
SOUTH COAST
TUSCANY
UNITED ARAB EMIRATES
USA SOUTHWEST
VENICE
VIENNA
VIETNAM

- PACKED WITH INSIDER TIPS
- BEST WALKS AND TOURS
- FULL-COLOUR PULL-OUT MAP AND STREET ATLAS

ROAD ATLAS

The green line ▬ indicates the Trips & Tours (p. 88–91)
The blue line ▬ indicates The perfect route (p. 30–31)

All tours are also marked on the pull-out map

Photo: Alphonse Beach

Exploring the Seychelles

The map on the back cover shows how the area has been sub-divided

A
B
C
1
2
3
4
5
6
L'Îlot (North Islet)
North Point
Carana Bay
Carana Beach
Machabée
Les Manguiers
Mahé
Vista do Mar
Montagne Glacis
Mt. Howard 458 m
Mont du Nord
Anse Nord
Glacis
Hodoul
Montagne Pigeon
Kreol Fleur
North East Point 119 m
Mon Plaisir
La Gogue
St. Antoine Estate
North
Sunset Beach
Glacis
Niederlande
La Gogue Village
La Retraite
La Gogue Road
Anse Étoile
Manresa
Pointe Cedre
Hilton Seychelles Northolme
La Gogue Reservoir
Nêzet
Maldive Village
Anse Étoile
F.E.B.A. Broadcasting Station
Hangard 374 m
Pti Payot
DE QUINCY
Loizeau
Mare Anglaise
Mont Signal 417 m
La Bastille (Ministry of Culture and Information)
Pointe Conan
Vallon Beach
Romance Guesthouse/ Bungalows
Mon Plaisir
Pointe Conan
Union Vale
Crève Coeur 388 m
Mt. Buxton
Coco d'Or Guesthouse
Beau Vallon Bay
Greenwich
Sun Resort
C & W Satellite Station
Cathedral of the Immaculate Conception
Castor St.
5th June Ave.
Pascal Village
St. Louis Minor 232 m
Bélonie
Victoria Helistop
Sullivan
Mare Anglaise
Yellow Gallery
St. Paul's Cathedral
VICTORIA
Dardanelles
Le Niol Road
Le Niol
Le Niol Waterworks
Dans Cedres
Russia
Bel Air Cemetery
Bel Air
Bel Air
State House
Le Chantier
Inner Harbour
Latanier Rd.
Port Office
Botanical Garden
Bel Eau
Pied du Morne
Mont Fleuri Rd.
Victoria Hospital
Sunrise
Mont Fleuri
Hermitage
Trois Frères Nature Trail
Mont Coton
Trois Frères 699 m
119
China
Sans Souci
Morne Seychellois National Par

D
E
F
1
1 km
0.62 mi
Indian Ocean
2
Praslin
3
Anse Cabot
Grand' Anse
Battery
Sainte Anne
250 m
Gr Manon
Albert
Grand Manon
4
Sainte Anne
Petit Manon
Anse Manon
Sainte Anne Resort
Anse Cimitière
Anse Mare Jupe
Old Whaling Station
Ste. Anne Channel
Moyenne Island
Cemetery & Ruins
(Île Moyenne)
a Lighthouse
Sainte Anne Marine National Park
5
Jolly Rogers
Round Island
(Île Ronde)
Long Island
(Île Longue)
Cerf Island Marine Park Resort
Cemetery
um
Cerf L'Habitation
108 m
6
Cerf Island
(Île au Cerf)
Eden Island
Cerf
Île Cachée

121

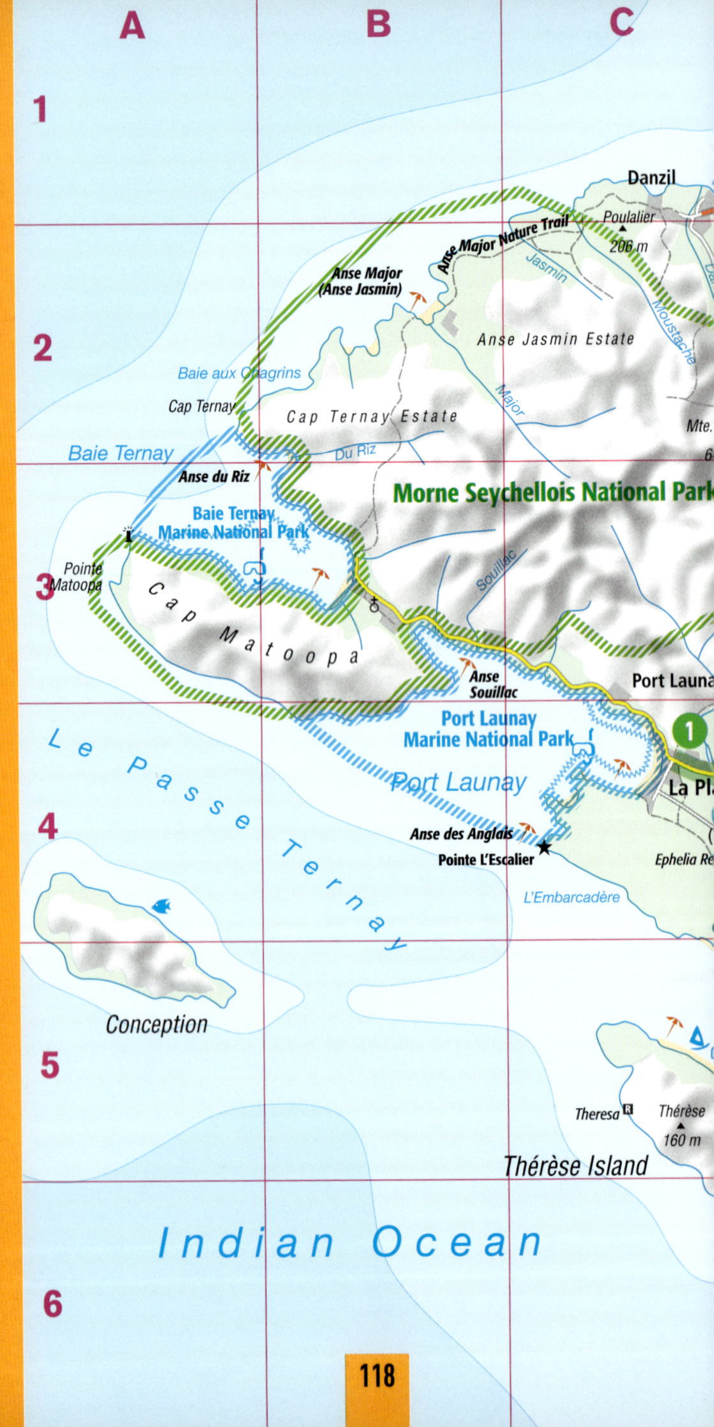
A
B
C
1
2
3
4
5
6
Danzil
Poulalier
206 m
Anse Major Nature Trail
Jasmin
Anse Major
(Anse Jasmin)
Anse Jasmin Estate
Moustache
Baie aux Chagrins
Cap Ternay
Cap Ternay Estate
Major
Mte.
Baie Ternay
Du Riz
Anse du Riz
Morne Seychellois National Park
Baie Ternay
Marine National Park
Pointe
Matoopa
Cap Matoopa
Souillac
Anse
Souillac
Port Launay
Marine National Park
Le Passe Ternay
Port Launay
Anse des Anglais
Pointe L'Escalier
Ephelia
L'Embarcadère
Conception
Theresa
Thérèse
160 m
Thérèse Island
Indian Ocean

Beau Vallon Bay
BEAU VALLON
Beau Vallon Beach
Romance Guesthouse Bungalows
116
Coral Strand
Petit Port
Le Méridien Fisherman's Cove
Berjaya Beau Vallon Bay
Coco d'Or Guesthouse
Sun Resort
Crève Coeur
388 m
Mt. Buxton
C & W Satellite Station
Cathedral of the Immaculate Conception
BEL OMBRE
St. Roch
Sullivan
Mare Anglais
Pascal Village
St. Louis Minor
232 m
Bélonie
St. Paul's Cathedral
Le Niol
Yellow Gallery
Dardanelles
Le Niol Road
Le Niol Waterworks
Dans Cedres
Russia
Bel Air Cemetery
Bel Air
Athanas
Mamzelle Anna
Grand St Louis
Botanical Garden
Pied du Morne
Victoria
Mont Le Niol
681 m
Trois Frères Nature Trail
Mont Coton
3
Trois Frères
699 m
Mare aux Cochons
Morne Seychellois National Park
Pérard
Morne Seychellois
905 m
Gongo Rouge
L'Exil
Mont d'Or
Forêt Noire
Casse Dent
Sans Souci Road
Griffiths
L'Oiseau
Morne Blanc
667 m
Mission Historical Ruins
L'Islette
Sauzier
Grand Bois
Antat
Dugand
Port Glaud
Agricultural Station
Forêt Noire Rd.
Désert
Grand'Anse
L'Islette
Seychelles Tea & Coffee Company (Tea Factory)
Cephale
Mt Posée
Petite Île
Glaud
Berjaya Mahé Beach Resort
Montagne
La Béolière
Grand' Anse
Agricultural Station
Grand' Anse
Les Trois Dames
1 km
0.62 mi
49 m
Île aux Vaches
Mahé

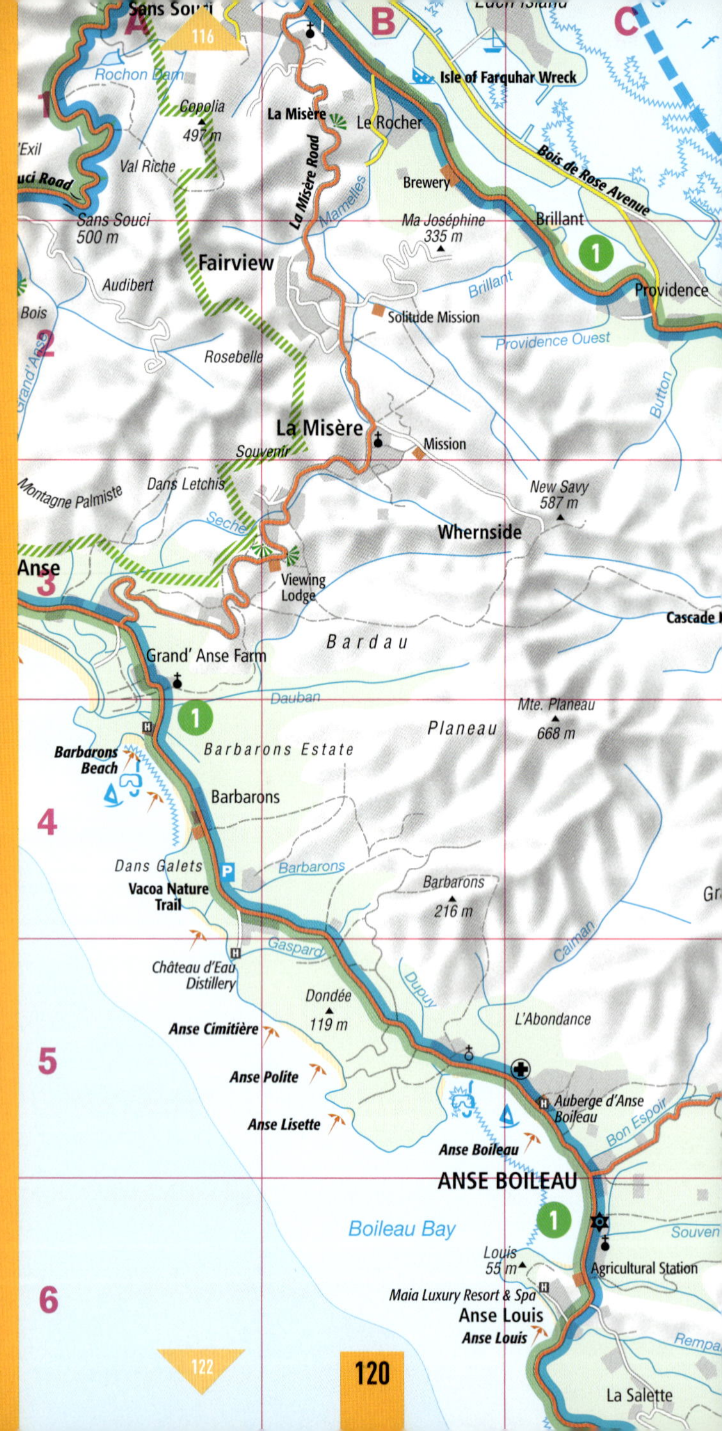

116
A
B
C
1
2
3
4
5
6
Sans Souci
Rochon Dam
Copolia
497 m
'Exil
uci Road
Val Riche
Sans Souci
500 m
La Misère
Le Rocher
La Misère Road
Mamelles
Brewery
Isle of Farquhar Wreck
Bois de Rose Avenue
Ma Joséphine
335 m
Brillant
Providence
Fairview
Audibert
Bois
Grand'Anse
Rosebelle
Solitude Mission
Providence Ouest
Button
La Misère
Mission
Souvenir
Montagne Palmiste
Dans Letchis
Seche
New Savy
587 m
Whernside
Anse
Viewing
Lodge
Cascade
Bardau
Grand' Anse Farm
Dauban
Mte. Planeau
668 m
Planeau
Barbarons Estate
Barbarons
Beach
Barbarons
Dans Galets
Vacoa Nature
Trail
Barbarons
Barbarons
216 m
Gr
Caiman
Gaspard
Château d'Eau
Distillery
Dupuy
Dondée
119 m
L'Abondance
Anse Cimitière
Anse Polite
Anse Lisette
Auberge d'Anse
Boileau
Bon Espoir
Anse Boileau
ANSE BOILEAU
Boileau Bay
Souven
Louis
55 m
Agricultural Station
Maia Luxury Resort & Spa
Anse Louis
Anse Louis
Rempa
La Salette
122

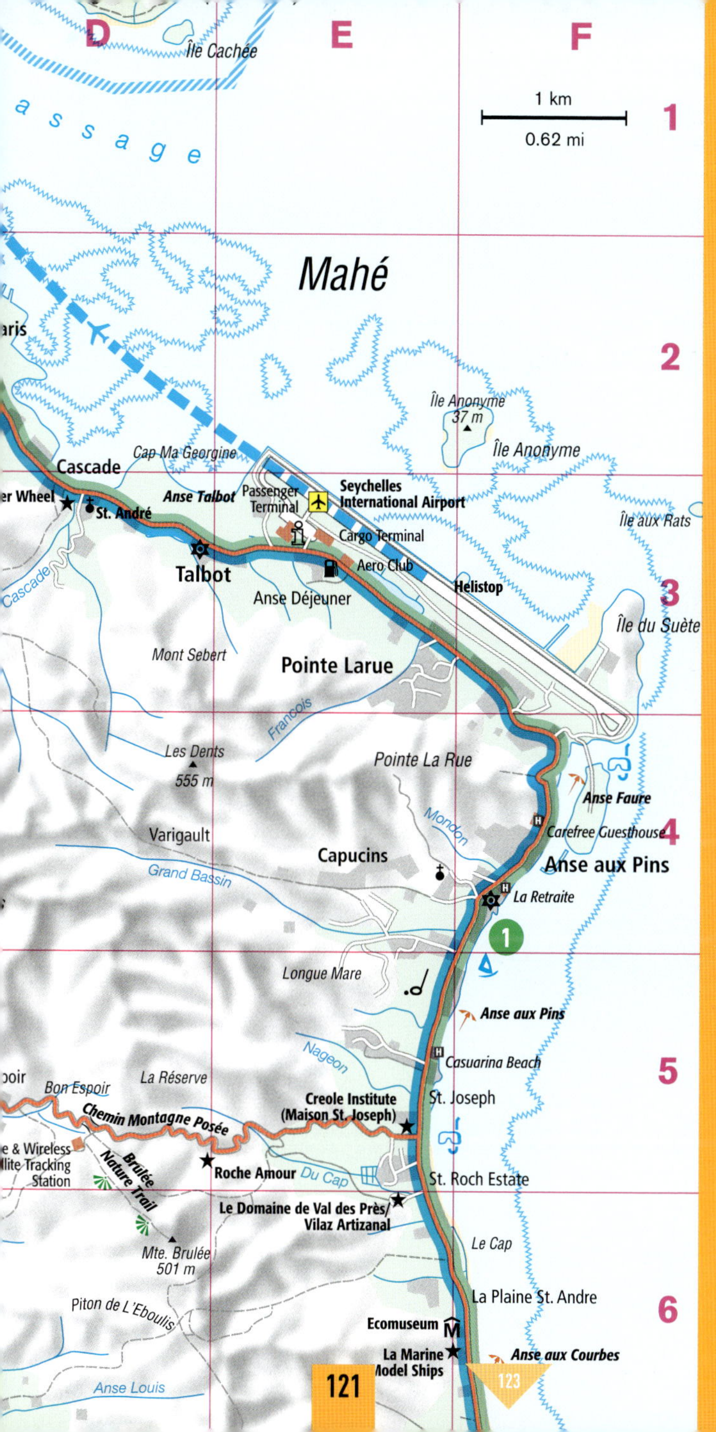
D
E
F
Île Cachée
assage
1 km
0.62 mi
1
Mahé
2
Île Anonyme
37 m
Île Anonyme
Cap Ma Georgine
Cascade
Anse Talbot
Passenger Terminal
Seychelles International Airport
St. André
Île aux Rats
Cargo Terminal
Talbot
Aero Club
Helistop
3
Anse Déjeuner
Île du Suète
Cascade
Mont Sebert
Pointe Larue
Francois
Les Dents
555 m
Pointe La Rue
Anse Faure
Mondon
Carefree Guesthouse
4
Varigault
Capucins
Anse aux Pins
Grand Bassin
La Retraite
1
Longue Mare
Anse aux Pins
Nageon
Casuarina Beach
5
La Réserve
Bon Espoir
St. Joseph
Creole Institute (Maison St. Joseph)
Chemin Montagne Posée
Brûlée Nature Trail
Roche Amour
Du Cap
St. Roch Estate
Le Domaine de Val des Près/ Vilaz Artizanal
Le Cap
Mte. Brulée
501 m
La Plaine St. Andre
6
Piton de L'Eboulis
Ecomuseum
La Marine Model Ships
Anse aux Courbes
Anse Louis
123

A
B
C
120
1
2
3
4
5
6
Dans Gravier
Jardin des Palmes
L'Esperance
Anse à la Mouche
Les Canelles Road
Anse à la Mouche
Villa Bambou
Blue Lagoon
Tom Bowers Studio
Chauve Souris
Anse aux Poules Bleues
Anse Soleil
Roche Soleil
125 m
Studio von Sir Michael Adams
Anse Soleil
Anse Soleil Beachcomber
Roche Gratte Fess
Anse aux Poules Bleues
Anse Soleil Road
Dame le Roi Road
Petite Anse
St. François d'Assisie
Four Seasons
Baie Lazare Village
Mte. Toupie
200 m
Val Mer
Val d'Endor
Baie Lazare
Baie Lazare
Anse Gaulettes
Anse du Gouvernement
Anse Gaulettes
Mte. Maravi
221 m
Lazare Picault
Val d'Endor Es
Petite Gouvernement
Pointe Lazare
Pointe Maravi
Li-al-do Maison
Mahé
Takamaka
Anse Takamaka
Villas Chez Batista
Le Réduit
Banyan Tree Hotel
Roche de l'Intendance
Anse Intendance
Indian Ocean
Pointe Go
1 km
0.62 mi

D
E
F
121
1
2
3
4
5
6
ont Plaisir
Moripa
T. Butler
Piton Jean Marie
(Oliver Hill)
232 m
Pointe au Sel
Fairyland
Pointe au Sel
Monte Cristo
St. Antoine
Le Relax
Souris
Kaz Kreol
Anse Royale
Royale
Anse Royale
Sweet Escott Road
Anse Royale
Bay
Le Jardin du Roi
Désert
330 m
Terrain Maillet
Anse Baleine
Bougainville
Anse Bougainville
d'Endor Road
Bougainville
Anse Parnel
Mont Parnel
378
Cap Lascar
Clovis
Cap Lascars
(Cap Maçons)
Anse Forbans
Chalets d'Anse Forbans
Anse Forbans
Anse Marie Louise
atre Bornes
Anse Marie Louise
Intendance
Quatre Bornes
Petite Marie Louise
Beau Séjour
301 m
Robert
Mont Cauvin
Collines du Sud
Mte.
Corail
Pointe
Capucins
Anse Capucins
Grande Police Road
Grande Police
Giraffe
Montagne Capucines
Pointe
Cocos
e Corail
Anse Bazarca
Petite Police
Petite Boileau
Police Bay
Police Point
Pointe du Sud
(Cap Malheureux)

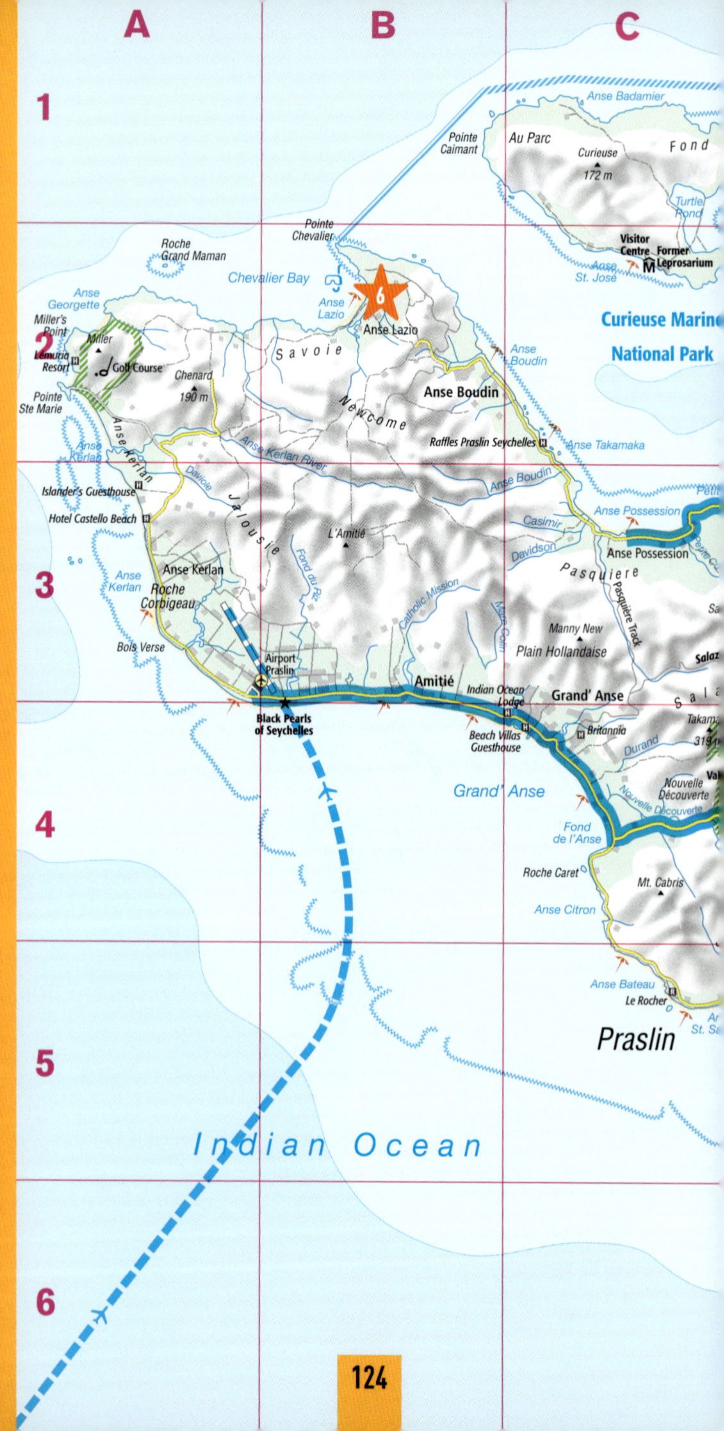
A
B
C
1
2
3
4
5
6
Anse Badamier
Pointe Caimant
Au Parc
Curieuse
172 m
Fond
Turtle Pond
Visitor Centre
Former Leprosarium
Anse St. José
Pointe Chevalier
Roche Grand Maman
Chevalier Bay
Anse Lazio
Anse Lazio
Anse Georgette
Miller's Point
Miller
Lemuria Resort
Golf Course
Chenard
190 m
Pointe Ste Marie
Savoie
Newcome
Anse Boudin
Anse Boudin
Curieuse Marine National Park
Raffles Praslin Seychelles
Anse Takamaka
Anse Kerlan
Anse Kerlan
Anse Kerlan River
Daviole
Islander's Guesthouse
Hotel Castello Beach
Jalousie
L'Amitié
Anse Boudin
Casimir
Davidson
Anse Possession
Anse Possession
Pasquiere
Pasquière Track
Anse Kerlan
Anse Kerlan
Roche Corbigeau
Fond du Riz
Catholic Mission
Mare Colin
Manny New
Plain Hollandaise
Bois Verse
Airport Praslin
Amitié
Indian Ocean Lodge
Grand' Anse
Black Pearls of Seychelles
Beach Villas Guesthouse
Britannia
Durand
Grand' Anse
Nouvelle Découverte
Nouvelle Découverte
Fond de l'Anse
Roche Caret
Mt. Cabris
Anse Citron
Anse Bateau
Le Rocher
Praslin
Indian Ocean

D
E
F
1
2
3
4
5
6
Pointe Rouge
Grand' Anse
Curieuse
Baie Curieuse
Île St. Pierre
Réserve Hotel
Laurier
Village du Pêcheur
Praslin Beach Hotel
Anse Volbert
Anse Volbert Village
Anse Matelot
Anse Gouvernement
L' Archipel Hotel
Côte d'Or
Côte d'Or Lodge
Villas d'Or
Casino des Îles
La Goulue
Pointe Joséphine
Fond Diable
213 m
Grand Anse
Midlands
Stooge
Entrance Gate
Viewing Lodge
National Park
Au Cap
Anse Takamaka
Anse La Blague
Île Malice
Anse Madge
Au Morne
Pointe La Farine
La Hauteur
Cap Samy
Anse Badamier
New Emerald Cove Hotel
Anse La Farine
Round Island
75 m
Baie Ste. Anne
Praslin
367 m
Baie Ste. Anne
Anse L'Amour
Eve Island
Round Island (Île Ronde)
Pélissier
Ferry
La Digue
Côté Mer Hotel
Colibri Guesthouse
Fond Ferdinand
Jenny
Pointe Cabris
Coco de Mer Hotel
Consolation
Anse Marie-Louise
Château de Feuilles
Roche Boquet
Anse Bois de Rose
Anse Marie Louise
Consolation
Anse Consolation
Anse Consolation
Pointe Cocos
1 km
0.62 mi
Mahe

A
B
C
1
2
3
4
5
6
Indian Ocean
Pointe La Verangue
Anse Mondon
Pointe Machabée
Camp Bloc
Anse Mondon
Grebau
Baie Cipailles
Belle Vue
Casse Tonnère
Dans L'Inde
Roche Marceline
Mare aux Cochons
Machabée
Dans Girofle
Anse La Passe
Grand Congoman
Silhouette Island
Special Reserve
Glacis Roullé
Pointe Cocos
Mont Pot à Eau
621 m
Mont Dauban
740 m
Grande
La Passe
Pointe Varreur
Pointe Etienne
Pointe Etienne
Jardin Marron
Mont Poules Marrons
Gratte Fesse
516 m
Mont Laurent
323 m
Anse Cimitière
Grande Machabée
Gratte Fesse
Rende D'Avance
Anse Lascars
Pointe Jardin
Quatre Cent
La Glacis
Anse Lascars
Pointe Zeng Zeng
Mont Corgat
Anse Grand Barbe
Grand Barbe
Anse Patates
Petite Passe
Mont Cocos Marrons
Silhouette
Coco dans Trou
Trevor
88 m
1 km
0.62 mi
Pointe Grand Barbe
Glacis Platte
Glacis Cocos Marrons
Pointe Civine
Indian
Grand Passe
Passe Johnny
Anse Cèdres Opark
Île Picard
Île Malabar (Middle Island)
Pointe du Nord
Île Polymnie
Aldabra Station (Research Station)
Grande Poche
Passe Femme
Passe Émile
Passe Yangue
Passe Magnon
Lagoon
Île Esprit
Île Moustique
Anse l'Ibis
Gros Îlot
Grande Terre (South Island)
Anse Quive
Anse aux Vacoas
Pointe Rien Fin

D
E
F
1
2
3
4
5
6
La Digue
1 km
0.62 mi
Anse Patates
L'Ocean Hotel
Anse Sévère
Patatran Bungalows
Anse Gaulettes
Cap Barbi
Cemetery
Le Domaine de l'Orangeraie
Anse Grosse Roche
Cap Bayard
Le Tournesol
Le Calou
Anse Banane
La Passe
Bernique
Fleurs de Lys
Grégoire's
La Digue Island Lodge
Ferry
Le Château St. Cloud
Paradise Flycatcher's Lodge
Pension Michel
Anse Fourmis
Anse La Réunion
Veuve Reserve
Nid d'Aigle
333 m
Anse Caiman
Copra Factory
L'Union Bungalows
Roche Bois
Fond Piment
Pointe Ma Flore
L'Union Estate
Anse Cocos
Source d'Argent
Pointe Source d'Argent
Citadelle
150 m
La Retraite
Anse Source à Jean
Petite Anse
Pointe Bélize
Grand' Anse
Anse Pierrot
Pointe Canon
Anse aux Cèdres
Grande L'Anse
Anse Bonnet Carré
Grand Cap
Indian Ocean
Pointe Jacques
Anse Marron
Anse Bambou
Anse Maquereau
Frégate Island Lodge
Anse Victorin
Pointe Fouqué
Frégate
Signal Rock
125m
Plantation House
Grand' Anse
Pointe Sud
Petite Grand' Anse
Anse Parc
0,5 km
0.31 mi
Anse Felix
Anse Coup de Poing
ean
Passe Houareau
Anse Cèdres
Île aux Cédres
Île Michel
Anse Takamaka
Anse Mapou
Aldabra Atoll
5 km
3.1 mi

KEY TO ROAD ATLAS

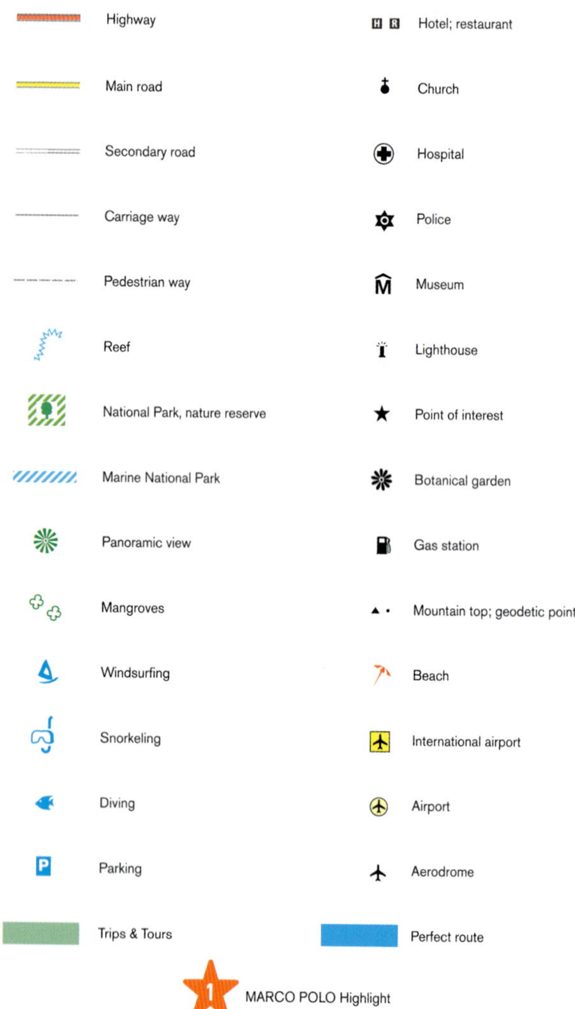

INDEX

This index lists all islands, towns and bays as well as names and key words featured in this guide. Numbers in bold indicate a main entry.

WRITE TO US

e-mail: info@marcopologuides.co.uk

Did you have a great holiday?
Is there something on your mind?
Whatever it is, let us know!
Whether you want to praise, alert us to errors or give us a personal tip – MARCO POLO would be pleased to hear from you.
We do everything we can to provide the very latest information for your trip. Nevertheless, despite all of our authors' thorough research, errors can creep in. MARCO POLO does not accept any liability for this. Please contact us by e-mail or post.

MARCO POLO Travel Publishing Ltd
Pinewood, Chineham Business Park
Crockford Lane, Chineham
Basingstoke, Hampshire RG24 8AL
United Kingdom

PICTURE CREDITS
Cover photograph: African Coast: Getty Images: Digital Vision (Buena Vista Images)
Tom Bowers (16 centre); DuMont Bildarchiv: Huber (30 left, 5051, 67, 90, 103); Holger Ehlert (16 bottom); Getty Images: Digital Vision (Buena Vista Images) (1 top); H. Gstaltmayr (1 bottom, 4, 28, 48); Huber: Johanna Huber (44), Mehlig (2 centre bottom, 32/33), Ripani (62), Schmid (front flap right, 22, 24/25, 37); © iStockphoto.com: Ian McDonnell (17 top); R. Jung (2 bottom, 7, 10/11, 52/53, 61, 99, 129); KREOLOR LTD: Gilbert Pool (16 top); Laif: Aurora (Clajot) (73), hemis.fr (Degas) (18/19), Heuer (26 left), Kirchgessner (26 right), Le Figaro Magazine (Fautre) (82), Martin (54, 76, 106); La Terra Magica: Lenz (front flap left, 30 right, 58, 96, 102 bottom); Look: age fotostock (2 centre top, 8, 98/99), Nordic Photos (97); mauritius images: Alamy (3 centre, 65, 74/75), ib (Moxter) (34, 88/89); H. Mielke (2 top, 3 top, 3 bottom, 5, 9, 12/13, 28/29, 29, 40/41, 43, 68/69, 79, 80/81, 85, 87, 92/93, 94, 98, 102 top, 114/115); P. Spierenburg (6, 15, 20, 27, 39, 47, 56, 70); Wilderness Safaris: Dana Allen (17 bottom)

1st Edition 2013
Worldwide Distribution: Marco Polo Travel Publishing Ltd, Pinewood, Chineham Business Park, Crockford Lane, Basingstoke, Hampshire RG24 8AL, United Kingdom. Email: sales@marcopolouk.com

Chief editors: Michaela Lienemann (concept, managing editor), Marion Zorn (concept, text editor)
Author: Heiner F. Gstaltmayr; editor: Jochen Schürmann
Programme supervision: Anita Dahlinger, Ann-Katrin Kutzner, Nikolai Michaelis
Picture editors: Gabriele Forst, Barbara Schmid
What's hot: wunder media, Munich
Cartography road atlas & pull-out map: DuMont Reisekartografie, Fürstenfeldbruck; © MAIRDUMONT, Ostfildern
Design: milchhof : atelier, Berlin; Front cover, pull-out map cover, page 1: factor product munich
Translated from German by Nicole Meyer; editor of the English edition: Margaret Howie, fullproof.co.za
Prepress: M. Feuerstein, Wigel
Phrase book in cooperation with Ernst Klett Sprachen GmbH, Stuttgart, Editorial by Pons Wörterbücher

Printed in China.

DOS & DON'TS

A few things to look out for on your Seychelles holiday

DO DRIVE WITH CAUTION

Mahé, the main island, is fun to discover by car but a word of caution: driving under the influence can quickly turn your adventure into a dangerous outing. Many roads lack guard rails and shoulders and have steep drops instead. In addition many locals have a driving style that affords little consideration to the visitor.

DO OBEY NATURE CONSERVATION RULES

It is a given that you always take your rubbish with you when leaving the beach and obey the 'No Smoking' signs – such as in the Vallée de Mai on Praslin. Smoking poses a real danger, especially in the dry months. Hiking trails are signposted, so keep to the path to avoid trampling on protected plants. And a request to divers and snorkellers: marine creatures, especially corals, should remain where they are.

DON'T GIVE THIEVES AN OPPORTUNITY

In recent years minor thefts and scams have increased on a small scale and there are even reports of cars being broken into. It is therefore best that you don't carry more money than is necessary and never leave valuables – mobile phones and cameras – in the car. And never display a bulging wallet ...

DON'T IGNORE SWIMMING SIGNS

Red danger signs on the beaches indicate that swimming is not allowed or warn of dangerous currents and these signs should never be ignored. These signs are there with good reason as these currents regularly claim lives.

DO AVOID SOUVENIRS MADE FROM TORTOISESHELL

Once you have seen how the shell is removed from a tortoise, you would voluntarily forego buying souvenirs made of tortoise shell. Unfortunately these products, which are banned in the Seychelles, are still sold in some shops. Besides, importing products that derive from protected animals or plants is a punishable offense in EU countries and the USA.

DON'T DISTURB RELIGIOUS EVENTS

Imagine a group of tourists barging into a service at your church and taking pictures while you are saying the Lord's Prayer! It should be a given that you do not to disturb religious gatherings in this way. And yet there are still people that find a church with believers more photogenic than one without. Taking pictures in front of the church is not a problem, the Seychellios are usually happy to oblige.